Mastering Move

Mastering Movement
The Life and Work
of Rudolf Laban

JOHN HODGSON

A Theatre Arts Book
Routledge
New York

1 3 5 7 9 10 8 6 4 2

Published in the U.S.A. and Canada in 2001 by
Routledge
29 West 35th Street
New York, NY 10001
www.routledge-ny.com

By arrangement with Methuen Publishing Ltd.

Cataloging-in-Publication data
is available from
the Library of Congress

ISBN 0 87830 080 5

Typeset by Deltatype Ltd, Birkenhead, Merseyside

Printed and bound by
Creative Print and Design (Wales), Ebbw Vale

Publisher's Note

John Hodgson died in June 1997 shortly after completing the final draft of this book. For over twenty years, John had been amassing probably the single most important archive of material by and about Laban and this study had been the focus of many long years of thought and toil. So we are pleased that its publication will stand as a fitting tribute to all his efforts. As the reader will learn, understanding Laban is no easy task. This book is about a search and the effort of grappling with a creative spirit who seemed to defy rational exposition. Yet John's researches and interpretation allow future generations of practitioners and scholars to view Laban with fresh eyes, and in understanding Laban, he probably came to understand more about the many different strands of his own full life.

We are very grateful to Donald Howarth and Vivien Bridson for their generous assistance in preparing John's manuscript for press and ensuring that his life's work now contributes to the further understanding of Laban's genius.

Contents

Preface: Laban in Question

Rudolf Laban (1879–1958) was a remarkable individual. He arguably had (and is still having) more influence than any other single figure in several fields of human activity: contemporary dance and dance training, the foundations of actor training, attitudes towards physical education, the development of dance and drama therapy, as well as methods of personnel selection and training in the work-place. For most people, just influencing one of these areas would seem enough. To be a dance practitioner or theorist or an inventor of a notation system for movement would have been a satisfying achievement. But Laban embraced all of these fields and found no conflict. There was one thing which united his many, seemingly diverse interests: he devoted himself to the understanding of what he saw as their common denominator – human movement. What he attempted to do in all these fields was to master movement.

Several people before him had worked out theories of movement in their specialist areas and left behind various philosophies and movement systems. No one, however, before or since Laban has provided the basis from which it is possible to see the relationship between such diverse physical activities. Laban's theory of movement takes ideas an important step further; it is both holistic and universal. It enables man to gain greater understanding of himself and his place in the world.

So why is Laban's work not better known? Why does there remain so much confusion and doubt about what exactly he has to offer? Collecting materials and information towards writing a life of Laban for over two decades has led me not only to a greater realization of the value of his work, but also to appreciate how complex and difficult it is for anyone to grasp the overall significance of his practice and gain anything like a coherent view of his theory. For me, it was a long journey towards understanding Laban.

At first, the most important sources of information about Laban seemed to come from people who lived and worked with him. Yet it was here that problems immediately became evident. Those who knew him discovered different aspects of the man: some who had known him intimately at one stage in his life had little appreciation of areas he had explored at other points. Some who knew him well and personally during his later life could hardly believe he had been such a different man, following apparently different aims, when younger.

Laban and his influence travelled widely. My enquiries led me to the Czech Lands and Slovakia, Austria, Switzerland, the former East and West Germany, and elsewhere through-out Europe, to the United States and even to South Africa. Scholars and practitioners (several themselves also under-taking in-depth studies on Laban) came to me with questions from a number of European countries, from North and South America, from Scandinavia and Japan.

Two world wars and all his continuous travelling left a cold trail since few earlier papers or research materials have survived, although some archives, stored since 1937, in Eastern Germany*, turned up in the late 1970s and helped to fill in important gaps. People who knew Laban generally thought so highly of him that they were most generous with time and memorabilia. But it was always fascinating to find that they too had questions about the man and his work.

As time passed and a more coherent picture of Laban emerged, I began to piece together themes, theories and concepts about him and regularly tested my understanding against Laban's fellow practitioners and friends. Some

---

* Now housed in the Dance Archive, Leipzig.

readily agreed, some questioned and modified my views and not a few vehemently denied my premise one day, only to return a day or two later to declare generously, 'You know, I think you are right.'

It is never easy to clarify anyone's life's work but it is especially problematic with such a complicated, varied and traumatic life as that of Laban. The fact that he lived in so many countries, conversed in so many languages, worked under so many political regimes and became involved in so many areas of human endeavour have made it a long and difficult task to identify patterns, recognize recurring themes and interpret basic principles.

Being involved with the material for so many years, I have found myself going through all kinds of attitudes towards it, only to emerge again and again with renewed enthusiasm and an even more positive realization of the value and importance of it all. I have lectured about Laban to all sorts of people in all kinds of places, held tutorials on his work, constantly applied and practised his theory and dined out on anecdotes on scores of occasions. The response of listeners has been one of considerable interest and always a desire to know more about him.

Sometimes questions have been quite fundamental. What are Laban's theories? Is there a Laban method one can delineate? Or some, assuming one to exist, wished to have details about it. How does Laban's theory relate to practice? How much did he practise? In what areas? How did he develop his ideas? Where did he get his ideas from? Who helped him and in what ways? Why is his work important? Why do some people know only about one aspect (usually Labanotation*) and sometimes refuse to accept that his work reaches into many other spheres?

Some of my listeners were quite specialist in their questions – 'I'm a teacher of drama. How can Laban assist me?' 'Tell me,' a West End theatre director once said, 'in

---

* Also technically known as *Kinetographie Laban*.

what ways can Laban help the actor in a play? What has Laban to say to the director?'

Or sometimes questions were framed another way: 'Laban's all very well for educational dance, but he has nothing to offer the young professional or would-be professional dancer, has he?' Or, 'I want to get to know what Laban has to offer, where should I start my understanding?'

Because it is not possible to give a simple, brief answer to any of these enquiries, I decided at least to attempt to select some of the more salient factors which have emerged as a result of researching and studying Laban's life and work, and to set them down in as clear a form as practicable so as to be helpful to a wide range of future practitioners: dancers and choreographers, actors and directors, teachers, therapists and movement specialists of all kinds.

This book represents my journey, attempting to establish Laban's basic ideas and the significance of these ideas in practice, based on a sound understanding. It is divided into an Introduction and five sections: The Introduction faces the question of why Laban was so well known in his lifetime and so comparatively little known afterwards. Part I identifies the problems which seem to stand in the way of understanding and clarifying Laban's theory. Parts II and III consider the evidence on which a better understanding can be based: in Part II, the circumstantial evidence and in Part III, the documentary. Part IV attempts a clarification of Laban's main ideas and Part V indicates some ways and areas in which these can be applied today.

Though my book will not satisfy all, it is offered in the hope that it will form a useful basis for a good many and a vital starting-point from which to make important discoveries.

John Hodgson
London 1996

Acknowledgements

A book that has been on its way for over twenty years is likely to have seen much change and development and to have encountered many people and situations that have influenced, assisted, blocked or stimulated its progress.

Generally I met with extremely generous support and encouragement to complete the project. I am grateful to all who have been associated with it, including many students and ex-students who have undertaken dogsbody work of filing and cataloguing. I wish to thank especially Ian Taylor who beavered away over a number of years and Eve Luddington who typed out an entire draft from my almost unreadable longhand. My thanks are also due to Vivien Bridson who was so helpful in those early days when I was assembling material and finding my way through Laban territory.

The first draft of the present manuscript was read by two people who made many useful comments: Dr Valerie Preston-Dunlop at the Laban Centre brought her knowledge and scholarly eye, pointing out errors and raising questions of fact; and Donald Howarth (playwright and theatre director) scrutinized the style and looked over almost every construction. Both of these proved most helpful contributions and challenged me to undertake yet another re-write.

Finally I would like to record my gratitude to Michael Earley at Methuen for his enthusiasm and publisher's perception shown both through his questions and his suggestions which greatly improved the book's layout and accessibility.

A Brief Chronology of Major Events in Laban's Life

(selected to relate to situations mentioned in the text)

1879: Born in Pozsony, Hungary (the town also known as Pressburg, Southern Bohemia and Bratislava, Slovakia). Son of Military Governor in Austro-Hungarian Empire.

1891: Several journeys (in this and subsequent years) to and with his father on military duties. Impressed by religious ceremonies.

1895: Apprenticed to local artist; access to and interest in local theatre.

1896: First journey to the Orient. Encounters the dancing of the Dervishes.

1899–1900: Military training in Vienna (Wiener Neustadt).

1900–1909: Married to Martha Fricke (painter, d. 1907). Short period in Munich, then to Paris. Painting and studying. Discovers François Delsarte's ideas on movement. Periods in Nice and Vienna. Experiments with movement, especially group improvisation.

1910: Married to Maja Lederer (singer). Lives in Munich until First World War. Working as painter and illustrator; studying notation systems and making further dance experiments.

1913: Runs summer school in Switzerland at Monte Verità, Ascona. Joined by Maja Lederer,

Suzanne Perrottet on staff; Mary Wigman arrives as student. Winter in Munich where he runs dance evenings and gives lectures and demonstrations.

1914:   Second summer in Ascona. Open-air performances. After outbreak of First World War, remains in Ascona working on space harmony and notation with Wigman.

1915–1919:   Moves to Zurich. Teaches, studies and sets up Laban School and 'Labangarten' for children. Laban students perform for the Dadaists at Cabaret Voltaire. Joined by Dussia Bereska. Starts work on *The Dancer's World*. Separation from Maja Lederer. Joins Bereska in Nuremberg.

1920:   Moves to Stuttgart with Bereska and opens Laban School. Publication of *The Dancer's World*.

1921:   Joined by Kurt Jooss, Albrecht Knust and others. Guest ballet-master at Mannheim National Theatre. Creates 'Bacchanale' for Wagner's *Tannhäuser* (Paris version).

1922:   Moves to Hamburg. Opens dance studio and theatre.

1923:   Officially opens theatre in buildings vacated by the zoo. Regularly premièring dance performances with leading roles often played by Laban himself. Company involved in productions in various other theatres throughout Hamburg. Pioneers the involvement of Speech and Movement Choirs with the dance.

1924:   Major tour taking the Tanzbühne Laban to Germany, Austria, Italy and Yugoslavia, which disbands in Zagreb due to financial collapse. Jooss and Sigurd Leeder to Munster to set up Neue Tanzbühne. Bereska sets up Laban School in Rome.

1925:   Tours with Gertrud Loeszer in duos based on Wagnerian characters.

1926:   Publication of *Children's Gymnastics and Dance*, *Gymnastics and Dance*, and *Choreography*. Three-

month tour to USA and New Mexico.
Choreographic Institute established in Würzburg.

1927: Choreographic Institute moved to Berlin alongside the Laban Central School. Arranges First Dancers' Congress at Magdeburg.

1928: Second Dancers' Congress, this time in Essen (Jooss organizes). Laban presents his notation system. Founds *Schrifttanz*, a journal devoted to discussion of dance writing.

1929: Directs pageants for Vienna Festival (involving 20,000 participants). Laban Central School moved to Essen (under Jooss's direction). Celebrates fiftieth birthday, with European dance periodicals running special articles and issues about him.

1930: At Bayreuth, running summer course with Wagner Festival. Première of 'Bacchanale' in Wagner's *Tannhäuser* (assisted by Jooss, Arturo Toscanini conducting). One-year appointment as ballet-master at the Berlin State Opera. Choreographic Institute moved to Essen.

1931: Again at Bayreuth. Revives 'Bacchanale' for Wagner Festival. Berlin State Opera appointment extended for three further years.

1932: Jooss's ballet *The Green Table* wins the International Choreographic Competition in Paris (with mainly classical jury).

1933: Hitler forms Nazi cabinet; Joseph Goebbels appointed Director of Reich Chamber of Culture.

1934: Jooss leaves Germany for England and sets up his company in Devon at Dartington Hall. Knust takes over direction of Central Laban School Folkwangschule at Essen. Hitler attends farewell matinée for Laban at Berlin State Opera. Becomes Director of Movement and Dance throughout Germany under Ministry of

Propaganda. Becomes a naturalized German Citizen.

1935: Organizes courses and promotes Dancers' Festivals (financed by the Nazis) for unemployed dancers. Begins Olympic dance competition organization inviting leading world dance figures. *A Life for Dance* published.

1936: Dress-rehearsal of *From the Warm Wind and the New Joy* in the Dietrich-Eckart-bühne at the corner of the main Olympic site attended by Goebbels who forbids performance. Runs International Dance Competition in Berlin. The Olympic Games open. Interrogated by police about his background. Resigns office; name and ideas forbidden to be used. Under 'house arrest' in Schloss Banz, Germany.

1937: Escapes to Paris.

1938: Becomes guest of Jooss and Leonard and Dorothy Elmhurst at Dartington Hall, England. Begins learning English, starts writing *Choreutics* and investigating three-dimensional abstract forms and Crystallography.

1939: Granted UK residency. Second World War declared. Jooss and Leeder interned.

1940: In London until bombing begins, then evacuated to Newtown, Wales, with Lisa Ullmann. Dance Notation Bureau founded in New York.

1941: With Ullmann, begins teaching at courses and conferences. Links with F.C. Lawrence on work-study methods in industry.

1942–1945: Moves with Lisa Ullmann to a new base in Manchester. Further courses on modern dance and work-study methods with growing range of industry.

1946: Art of Movement Studio opens in Oxford Road, Manchester.

1947: *Effort* (with F.C. Lawrence) published. Lectures and teaches throughout the country with some visits abroad

1948:   *Modern Educational Dance* published. *Laban Art of Movement Guild Magazine* begins publication. Joan Littlewood and Theatre Workshop move to Manchester. Art of Movement Studio gives first performances at Library Theatre, Manchester. Joins staff of Esme Church's Theatre School, Bradford.

1949:   Ministry of Education approves special course for Northern college lecturers

1950:   *Mastery of Movement on the Stage* published. Teaches with US faculty on American university theatre course at Dartington Hall, Devon.

1951:   Hands over direction of movement for York Cycle of Mystery Plays to Geraldine Stephenson because of illness. The *Observer* carries a profile on Laban. Juilliard School in New York requires Labanotation in new training programme.

1952:   Work starts to influence education, therapy and recreational courses.

1953:   The Studio moves to Addlestone, Surrey, to premises donated by William Elmhirst. Spends several months in hospital with typhoid fever. Begins work on *Movement Psychology* with William Carpenter.

1954:   Celebrates seventy-fifth birthday with special edition of *Guild Magazine.*

1955–1957:   Continues writing and teaching at the Studio and around the country. Laban Art of Movement Centre established in association with the Addlestone Studio.

1958:   Dies 1st July.

List of Illustrations

We are grateful to the John Hodgson Collection for permission to reproduce illustrations.

Introduction
LABAN'S INFLUENCE

'. . . Rudolf Laban's work in the theatre was a vital force throughout Europe . . .'

Susan Lester, former *Sunday Telegraph* dance critic

Introduction: Laban's Influence

Rudolf Laban's life and work span a remarkable period of political and artistic history. His experiences and movement discoveries extend from his childhood in Bohemia at the end of the nineteenth century, to his death in England in the middle of the twentieth. During his lifetime, both he and his ideas were world-renowned.

Influential Laban

At different periods of his life, Laban lived and worked in most of the artistic and political meccas of Europe: Sarajevo, Bratislava, Munich, Paris, Ascona, Prague, Hamburg, Budapest, Vienna, Zagreb, Berlin, Bayreuth and London. At one time or another, he worked with or for a range of people or institutions of considerable influence, including Hans Brandenburg, the Dadaists, Siegfried Wagner, Arturo Toscanini, Adolf Hitler, Joseph Goebbels, the British Ministry of Defence, Joan Littlewood's Theatre Workshop, and the British Ministry of Education. Between the wars there was hardly a major European city which did not have its Laban School.

He trained, influenced and/or developed the talents of a great many artists, including dancers like Mary Wigman (Marie Wiegmann), Gertrud Loeszer and Max Terpis; choreographers like Aurelio von Millos, Kurt Jooss and Geraldine Stephenson; theatre directors like David Giles and Joan Littlewood; and actors like Sir Robert Stephens, Bernard Hepton and Joan Plowright. The line of Laban's influence extends to pupils of pupils: individuals like Hanya Holm in her choreography of many Broadway musicals; Alwin Nicholai and Murray Louis, both with their own international dance companies; Pina Bausch, cult contemporary dance figure; British theatre directors Bill Gaskill, Peter Gill, David Scase and Philip Hedley; and fight director Malcolm Ranson.

He trained students who took his ideas into management consultancy, like that of Warren Lamb who passed ideas to his protégée Pamela Ramsden. He influenced people like Dr Irene Champernowne in her work at the Withymead Centre for Psychotherapy and his analysis of movement stimulated people like Veronica Sherborne, Walli Meier, Helen Payne and Susan Stockley in their practice of dance movement therapy.

Spread of Laban's Ideas

So much for name-dropping. Laban's ideas, however, have had an even greater general impact, through the work that he himself carried out and through the widespread influence of his theory and practice.

For many (including Oxford's *Concise Dictionary of Ballet*), his greatest and best-known contribution is Kinetographie Laban, or Labanotation as it has come to be known throughout the western world. His patented system for writing and recording movement by means of a series of signs and symbols enables all kinds of physical human activities to be accurately and fully recorded. His movement notation has been successfully employed to study and record almost every type of physical motion, from classical ballets to war or social dances; from the building of huge industrial boilers to the simple wrapping of a Mars candy bar.

Career on the Continent

Laban worked as a freelance artist for most of his life. From 1910 to the end of the 1920s, he ran his own school and dance companies. By the 1930s, he held important and prestigious artistic posts: he is credited with the choreography for a number of Wagnerian productions at the Bayreuth Festival; he became Director of Movement for the State Theatres in Berlin, which included the role of ballet-master at the Berlin State Opera; he became Director of the German Dance Theatre, in charge of movement and dance throughout Germany; and organized the international dance competition for the 1936 Olympic Games.

His dance theory and its practice throughout Europe established his reputation as the leader, father and founder of the Central European school of Modern Dance.

Moves to the United Kingdom

In 1938 Laban came to England as a refugee from Nazi Germany. Soon after, Britain was at war and the Nazi threat turned attention away from dance and drama training to defence. The dancer and choreographer had to diversify and, freelance once more, gradually found himself and his work gaining importance in a whole series of additional fields where the study of movement was essential. Although he had newly arrived from Germany, with the help of his patrons, the Elmhirsts, Laban escaped internment. He was soon making a contribution to the war effort and found himself being consulted by Sir John Slessor of the Air Ministry in the quest for greater troop safety and effectiveness in parachute-jumping.

On the home front, because most of the men had been called into the armed forces, jobs in industry and elsewhere had to be done by women. Many of the activities previously carried out by muscle and brawn now had to be done by people with quite different physiques. Help was needed to redirect this different work-force towards achieving the same productive ends. Laban became the expert consultant for all kinds of firms, including some involved with tyre manufacture, agriculture, tile works, sawmills, and confectionery.

Wartime Britain found Laban's approaches both stimulating and original. Schools, colleges and universities had, up to this point, mainly confined their fitness awareness to what was termed Physical Training. Some people had begun to argue that their responsibility should reach beyond strict exercise and line drill and towards a more holistic physical education. Laban's attitude towards bodily expression enabled education advisers, lecturers and teachers to follow their inclination with confidence, firmly basing their understanding on what they knew of his movement principles and theory.

Throughout the country, a new form of physical education developed, known as Modern Educational Dance, and Laban gathered a large following of (mainly female) proselytes from the specialist PT Colleges and elsewhere. There was a growing army of devotees throughout Britain whose experience on short and longer courses enabled them to appreciate the value of his work and to incorporate it in their own training programmes.

Peacetime Progress

The post-war years saw a boom in degree work and the need for clear, intelligible areas of study. Laban's work often became formalized and dogmatized for those in search of examinable material for dance and physical education. For a while, Laban theory became a bandwagon of academic respectability.

In more general education, too, his influence was felt. Occasionally a whole curriculum took on a different focus when all the work was built around expressive movement.

This transformed the atmosphere and even academic standards.

Throughout the final decade of his life, Laban extended his work into other fields of activity and followed those calls, where his time and energy permitted, into therapy and personal assessment. Managements grew to see the value of Laban's Effort Analysis and to observe how his approach went beyond the rather simplistic and mechanistic stopwatch appraisal to time and the work done within it. The general teacher shortage after the war was also demanding. The Ministry of Education financially encouraged all kinds of courses. Lisa Ullmann assisted Laban in developing his work in this field which extended into public (especially physical) education as Modern Educational Dance.

Adoption by the Theatre

In Bradford, in the North of England, Esme Church began her Northern Theatre School where she enrolled a number of students, including ex-servicemen. It was on a British Drama League weekend course that Esme Church first saw Laban teaching. She managed to persuade him to join her as director of movement. Laban, with one of his students, Geraldine Stephenson, regularly taught the actors movement and directed them in mime plays.

By 1946 the Laban Art of Movement Studio had opened in Manchester in the Oxford Road. Before long, and just across the way, Joan Littlewood and Ewan McColl established the house that became their headquarters for Theatre Workshop. This proved to be an opportunity for a fertile exchange of both services and ideas. Theatre Workshop incorporated movement classes into their rehearsal and workshop schedules and 'whenever possible', says Littlewood, 'we attended his studio', while the Art of Movement Studio derived the benefit of people like John Bury, their designer who later worked with Peter Hall at the Royal

Shakespeare Company, and of course Ewan McColl and Joan Littlewood themselves.

When the Art of Movement Studio moved in 1953 to its Addlestone home, the interest in actor training was at first small. Laban's later ideas, however, fired Yat Malmgren's imagination. He studied and utilized Laban theory in his teaching, first with students at the Central School of Speech and Drama, then at the Royal Academy of Dramatic Art and finally at the Drama Centre in London. Through such direct approaches and more indirect dissemination of Laban's ideas, it is hard to find any worthwhile movement training for actors in the UK at the present time that does not draw something from Laban's work, whether the influence is recognized directly or not.

Yet, in spite of all this activity, since his death Laban and his ideas seem to have carried far less influence. How can this be? I think there are answers to explain this eclipse in influence.

Part One

THE PROBLEMS IN UNDERSTANDING LABAN

'I worked with Hanya (Holm) . . . it was hard to distinguish what came from Wigman and what came from Laban . . .'

Alwin Nicholai, International Dance Director.

The Problems in
Understanding Laban

Ignored by Dance

Ironically, both before and since his death in 1958, the UK
and US dance worlds have given little credit to Laban's
work in their training and expression. It is odd that a one-
time choreographer to the Berlin State Opera and icon of
modern dance theory and notation technique should be so
little known within the professional dance fraternity.

Most will have heard of him, of course, but few will know
what he is about or be ready, or able, to acknowledge just
how much of the theory of this most influential dance figure
they are constantly using. Still fewer will realize fully what
more he has to offer them in understanding or extending
their appreciation and expression in dance.

Establishing a Permanent Centre

It was the movement education activity that enabled the
setting-up of an Art of Movement Studio, first in Manchester and then in Addlestone. The main emphasis (largely due
to financial pressures) was the training of movement
teachers, though there was a broader aim to provide an
International Centre for Research, Training and Teaching
of Movement Studies.

Things continued very much along the same lines right
through to 1972 when Lisa Ullmann, who had been the
Principal of the Art of Movement Studio since its inception,
retired. Finding a successor presented the trustees with a

considerable task since there had never been anyone else at the helm apart from Ullmann. During the early years, Laban himself had been a pervading presence but for the next fifteen Lisa Ullmann alone had operated supreme.

Return to the Dance

Dr Marion North, who had previously taught at the Art of Movement Studio, was appointed to succeed Lisa Ullmann. Dr North had worked closely with Laban as a research assistant. For a time Marion North held the appointment as Director of (now) The Laban Centre for Movement and Dance together with that of Head of Dance at the University of London's Goldsmith's College. This situation enabled Dr North to move the Centre into London in 1976, to a site adjacent to the Goldsmith campus. With the move came a significant shift of emphasis, once again, towards dance, with new staff and international links and outlook. It seemed that Laban's importance in the field of dance was about to be re-established. The wheel seemed to have come full circle and everything appeared exciting in its development and promising in its prospects.

Forgotten Laban

At the present time, there are but two institutions which carry his name: the Laban Centre for Movement and Dance in London and the Laban/Bartenieff Institute of Movement Studies in New York. Laban remains only a name with vague associations and recollections rather than being a towering, creative, iconic individual whose contribution is instantly recognized and whose worth is regularly accepted. Why are his ideas not more widely studied and applied in the movement-conscious world of today?

One reason springs from the very circumstances in which he lived and died. There is, it seems, an inevitable period after the death of many a well-known personality, be it politician, entertainer, writer or artist, when, in the process of establishing a more balanced perspective, a reputation passes through a period of discredit or eclipse. The individual is no longer there as a sharp reminder of all that he or she stands for and has influenced. Laban is no exception.

Reassessing Laban

With Laban's death and the years that have intervened, there are some people who have attempted to undertake a detailed scrutiny and devaluation of his work. He was a person of impressive bearing and authority. He also had a kind of remoteness which kept some at bay. Others, who might have had the gall or the boldness to approach him directly with criticism, were fended off, in a somewhat proprietary way, by a misguided few who surrounded him, seeking to protect Laban in deference to his age, his standing or his health.

Once he was dead, he could no longer be protected; nor could he protect himself. Reappraisal is useful, but the danger in such circumstances is that by our zeal for re-examination and critical re-evaluation, we too lose our objectivity. The temptation is to show we are thoroughly independent and so throw out Archimedes with the bath water.

Laban's case is unusual. When he died there were people who had worked with him in England, during the last twenty years of his career, but comparatively few who had spent any time with him in Europe during his first fifty. Amongst those surviving were individuals who had a long time been involved with their own versions of his theory and practice, and had become so engrossed in a single aspect that they had little time or inclination to seek or accept a broader view. It was the age-old problem of trying to maintain a perspective while working in close-up. Because of the aura of Laban the man, some claimed that through this closeness they had reached the fount of understanding and knowledge. The problem could only be recognized by bringing these ideas together so that it was possible to discern that it was rarely the same knowledge and hardly ever the same understanding.

Amongst his disparagers, on the other hand, there were those who were frustrated when they could not easily discover the answers. Some looked for a clear formula in Laban's life and work and blamed him if they could not readily find one. Some, regarding him as the Stanislavski of movement, wanted a system and looked for his equivalent of *An Actor Prepares* or *Building a Character*.

There were deprecators who maintained that Laban's ideas were restricted to limited fields of the dance or even to dance notation. Others wrote off dance notation as no longer relevant, claiming that now the job was done better by video. There were those who took some aspects of Laban's thinking and tested them against inappropriate criteria, seeking to prove themselves by finding him wanting. Some even set out to challenge the entire philosophical basis of his thinking.

The Quest and the Questions

How has all the confusion arisen? How can we arrive at any kind of clarification? Is it possible to gain an objective perspective? If we can forge a way through to the essential core of Laban's findings, leaving behind the admirers on the one hand and the detractors on the other, it should be possible to find where Laban's real worth lies.

Laban himself did not make it easy. He never attempted to present his theory with any degree of encyclopaedic wholeness. It becomes a matter of sifting and sorting a way through his activities, his principal contemporaries, his forerunners and his writings, towards a better understanding.

Before we can proceed on the main quest of the journey, we need to discover the principal factors which have brought about the break in the line of influence and understanding. So this is where we first begin.

1 The Fields of Laban's Enquiry

Laban himself is puzzling, so perhaps it is not so surprising to find that there are problems in understanding his work. A man of broad concerns and curiosity, he was never still. He changed his abode, his focus, his concentration, almost, it seems, with each new moon. Even in appearance he was perpetually modifying himself. There is something of the chameleon in the figure captured in photographs of him taken over the years. In one portrait he is an army officer cadet, in another he looks like a Bohemian poet. In one he looks more of a mystic, another presents him as a debonair young man, while a further photograph shows him rather like a business executive.

To some extent, the same changeability and expressive needs are reflected in his work. The range of his activity is often bewildering. Here we find him working as a stern dancing master, now he is the idealist, there the dancer, then the organizer, here the theoretician. At one point we find him writing songs in Paris. Now he is teaching on the slopes of a Swiss mountain, then on the telephone by his pageant-master's desk in Vienna, now at the Wagner Festival in Bayreuth, choreographing the ballet sequences in *Tann-häuser*, then designing a theatre, or painting a landscape by the Danube, or analysing workers' actions in factories in northern Britain.

His many talents and activities at different times and in different places have led some people to make extravagant claims that he was professional in any number of fields. There were those who believed him to hold a doctorate in medicine, and those who thought him to be qualified in quite a number of other disciplines. Joan Littlewood in her 'peculiar history', *Joan's Book*, gets carried away like so many others. 'I gathered,' she announces in her appendix on him, 'that he was or had been: a Dadaist, a crystallographer, topologist, architect . . . [and] while still in his twenties he had become the leading choreographer and dance master of the Weimar Republic.'[1]

How have these misconceptions taken root and where in all this does the truth lie? It almost seems that, at times, he was as much an enigma to himself as he was to others. At different periods of his life, he clearly sought to express in his outward guise and activity contrasting sides of his personality – or it may have been more of a search to discover it.

Parental Pressure

Being anybody's child and finding yourself is no easy task; finding your own identity as the son of a famous father is even harder. While Laban was still a schoolboy, at the end of the nineteenth century, his father was made first Deputy Governor, then Governor of Bosnia-Herzegovina. This was a military/diplomatic post and it was well known that the Emperor Franz Joseph personally hand-picked all his high-ranking officers.

The young Laban did not see much of his parents. Father was usually away on service and Mother, as often as not, went with him. Rudolf was sent away to school (where he tended to rebel) and visited his father in the holidays. While abroad with his father, he enjoyed physical exertion, found delight in the sports, and revelled in shooting, fencing and other forms of combat. He not only saw massive manœuvres of troops but sometimes took part in them himself, riding horseback alongside the young officers. He loved observing the formations of the troops and was never happier than when he saw musters, march-pasts and military parades.

Considering a Career

Though childhood and adolescence were surrounded by these military influences, there was another side to young Rudolf's personality which needed an outlet. He wanted and needed a more creative form of physical expression, so he found ways of releasing his feelings in and through performance. The family home was in Pozsony (later Bratislava), in southern Bohemia, and it was there, as he grew up, that he first became fascinated by puppet performances, and by the local theatre (for which his uncle held the keys). He also began to observe movement as a foundation of human expression – at funerals and weddings – and admired the deportment of women carrying pots on their heads.

Such were the pressures of his early life that he remained uncertain about a career until he was almost thirty. It was a tough world and one in which there was little room for compromise. Rudolf's father had been disappointed in his son's lack of success at school, but expected him to follow his father by taking up a military career. He was the eldest of four and the only son. Preconceptions about manliness only strengthened his father's endeavour and he brought more pressure to bear when it began to appear that his son was developing definite artistic leanings.

It was he who had shown him the troops in action, observed that Rudolf was a skilled horseman and so settled him at twenty as a cadet in the Officers' Training Academy at Wiener Neustadt (Vienna), fully anticipating that he would carry on the military line and enable the family at last to be proud of him. But Rudolf's heart, soul, and mind were not into the training. Instead of being interested in guns and mechanized equipment, his imagination perpetually wandered. He survived only by investing the inanimate instruments of war with a life of their own. 'For me it became clear that my place was not to serve the soulless steel-ox but rather to become a kind of adversary and antithesis to it, in spite of my admiration for its power.'[2]

The training establishment, though not Rudolf's father, realized that his talents lay elsewhere. Even at this stage, the young man thought of himself as an artist – though he remained confused as to exactly the kind of artist he might become. He endured the military academy for a full year, during which the only really happy time he had was when the authorities asked him to direct a dance festival of the cadets for the final celebration.

The return to his father with another failure created a greater rift between parent and child. Field Marshal Laban would not tolerate or attempt to understand his son's artistic leanings, let alone his tendency from time to time to express them in the clothes he wore. When he found his son insisting that art must be his life, his father advised him that if he could not, would not, change his ways, there was a gun in his desk drawer and that would at least be an honourable way out.

That remained a devastating experience for Laban and years after, he still felt that he could not go home until he had proved himself and his profession. What followed were phases in his development in which sometimes he was pulled towards the desire to display free expression and sometimes towards the determination to declare conventional respectability.

Permitted to Paint

Finally, however, his parents conceded that their son was not likely to follow his father's lead. So where was he to find a career? Parental pressures were still strong and when at last he convinced his father that he had to employ himself in the arts, his father insisted that it would have to be in the least controversial field; an art form which would have social acceptability. Rudolf had shown some talent in fine art, so it was reluctantly agreed that he should try his hand at painting. That art was acceptable even to the Popes. So, for almost a decade, he tried to forge a living as a painter and illustrator.

It was not until after his father died in 1907 that Laban's innate interest in dance had the opportunity to develop. Now almost twenty-eight, he began more seriously to give shape and direction to his former experiences, impressions, feelings and observations about movement and to use this understanding and awareness in a bid to build a more determined future in this field. The years until now had formed a kind of prelude, introducing themes, ideas and elements which would later be sorted out as principles, precepts or fundamental concepts.

Dance and dancing had always provided much of his greatest release and fulfilment. From his earliest days, he had known the delight of moving freely in the open air, seen the community spirit engendered in folk dance and witnessed the body control generated through dancing, whether in preparation for war or worship. His interest in its wider implications was already established: 'I gathered very early that it is the harmony of movement in leisure-time activities which is one of the main carriers of inner freedom and liveliness.'[3]

He had no formal training in the ballet, nor in any other form of dance. His training and experience in drawing and painting proved a useful means rather than an end in itself. In his thinking about dance, we find him applying his visual art experience. He knew that while there was delight in completing a canvas, there was even more to be derived when the pictures came to life.

From time to time, his painting teacher incorporated

young Rudolf's help in making some representational tableaux for special occasions or for visitors to his native Pressburg. But Laban's adrenalin really began flowing when he was assigned to arrange the pictures and make them move from one to the next.

Investigating Movement and Dance

While in Paris in his early twenties, Laban sold some of his graphics and managed to eke out the allowance given him from his father; he nevertheless continued to day-dream, hope and plan about dance and the theatre.

He studied at the Ecole des Beaux-Arts, exploring costume and theatre design. He examined early forms of dance-writing such as those of Thoinot Arbeau and Raoul-Auger Feuillet, all the time seeking a more accurate and all-embracing system that would record not just the steps or the floor pattern but the positioning of the body and the dynamic of the movement. He visited all kinds of entertainments and performed dances in the cabarets that thrived in Montmartre and elsewhere. His Parisian experiences of dance reinforced his feeling that dance should move away from theatrical pretence and pretension into the free and wholesome open air. He also spent time in Nice where he gathered together dancers and performers in an experimental arts community and made his first serious dance experiments.

It was not until he settled in Munich with his second wife, towards the end of the first decade of the twentieth century, that he began seriously to draw together his experiences. Everything was grist to the mill. With some memories and observations, he took a subjective response and wove fantasies which he shaped into scenarios for dances. With other recollections, he stood back more objectively, codifying them into philosophical bases and theory.

The two went hand-in-hand: as he worked on the dances

with groups and individuals, he continued to develop his theory and his practical application. His one-time student and co-worker, Mary Wigman recalled how the many facets of his activities really all led to one area of investigation.

> He was forced to make many detours and probably enjoyed branching off the main road from time to time, to investigate the more intimate side-streets and by-paths. But the original direction of his research was never changed by such diversions. The essential nature of his work might be caught in one word: movement.[4]

From shortly after the First World War until he suffered a back injury during a performance in 1926, Laban himself participated in the dances, both as principal dancer in his company and in duos on tour throughout Europe. He choreographed dozens of ballets for all sorts of occasions. He trained dancers, ran courses and taught large and small groups, and individuals.

In England from 1938 until 1958, his knowledge, under-standing and intuitive awareness took him into all kinds of other arenas where he was able to employ his concepts and theory. His work continued to expand. Laban, like many another individual with growing knowledge, realized, in spite of a lifetime's investigation, how much further there was to go. He remained a student, eager to find out more. Very late in his life as he saw the launching of the *Laban Art of Movement Guild Magazine*, he wrote:

> Grant me the privilege to try and to err, because trial and error is the basis of all healthy development.[5]

Though he had met frustration in following his chosen field of enquiry, Laban had the kind of personality which could make good use of almost any circumstances. As Laban moved his body, his mind moved also. He thought about those experiences of his earlier years and looked for connections. He related several of his past experiences to each other and examined where, how and when the body changed its position and considered the effects that moving has on the individual.

Drives in his Investigation

In the September 1951 edition of the *Laban Art of Movement Guild News Sheet*, he reflects on and identifies certain experiences and studies when confronted with the question, 'What has led you to study Movement?' It is possible to add to this from biographical study, additional experiences and to suggest that three main factors urged him forward.

The first was his own experience of dance as a fundamental and enriching activity. When he sorted the good from the bad, he knew the only times that had given him feelings of joy or a sense of satisfying creativity were those connected with dance and movement.

The second arose from the thoughtful, philosophical side to his nature linked with his basically optimistic attitude to life and the universe in which we live. He felt a desire, a *need* to make sense of it all. He knew he felt especially at one with things when he moved naked under the stars. Whatever it was that made people want to dance, he observed that it was a basic, human need. If there was anything at all in dancing, then it was not the superficial, escapist prostitute art that many non-dancers regarded it as being.

The third drive therefore was to prove to the world (and thus to his parents) that dance was and should be regarded as important, as respectable, with a standing and prestige equal to other art forms.

Gradually he began to clarify different aspects of movement, especially as they were expressed in all forms of dance. It was an ongoing process, making new observations, developing understanding and making new discoveries. From the beginnings in Munich and Ascona to his leaving Germany for Paris in 1938, his main focus is in the direct application of his findings to dance. But because of the fundamental nature of his investigations it was a comparatively easy task to relate his expertise to the broad field of human movement once he arrived in the UK.

2   The Nature of Laban's Thinking and Writing

Because Laban had such drive and ambition, it still seems odd that we should find it difficult to understand his ideas. A man who set himself the task of clarifying, codifying movement might be expected to have spent more time communicating a clear understanding of his findings. With so much examination of his notions by others, why is the understanding of his work not more straightforward? With so much refining of his concepts going on, why is much of his work inaccessible?

Visual, not Verbal, Thinking

Laban was never an academic or scholar. He never had any of the formal university training associated with scientific enquiry or research techniques; nor did he ever have the benefit of training in philosophic argument or logical reasoning. His formal education was limited.

Most people tend to test their intellect by confronting ideas (directly from another individual or via the written word) and sifting through the challenges offered. Some find discussion at home an important influence. For most, the educational patterns encountered derive from teachers at school and tutors at the university who can question findings and assumptions and debate the methods of approach employed. Laban found school so unconducive to thought that he spent very little time there. (He called his school attendances 'minimal guest appearances'.)[6] Apart from lectures at the École des Beaux Arts in Paris, he never really encountered the cut and thrust of academic discipline.

He was never even formally trained as a dancer. Much of his own dancing was intuitive, modified and extended by his observations, practical experience and understanding. He seems to have trained himself while he was training others. It is interesting to find him still, towards the end of his days, giving pride of place to 'trial and error' as 'the basis for all healthy development'.[7] The only problem was that he remained the main arbiter of what was effective trial and what might be conceived as undoubted error.

His only formal training was in drawing and painting. It is this broad yet informal practical education that seems most of all to have helped shape his thinking and condition his expression and communication. When he was still in his teens, in Bratislava, his parents agreed to his spending a good deal of his spare time with an old painter friend (whose name we do not know). He was a traditional artist of the naturalistic school. With his bristly, twirled moustache and distinct resemblance to Rembrandt, however, Laban clearly respected him – enough to confide in him as he did in few other adults.

Laban became his apprentice and through the old painter's guidance, Laban began to learn what he regarded as 'real craftsmanship'. After the dogsbody duties of cleaning brushes and setting out paints on his palettes, he learnt brush- and painting-techniques. This period of working with the master-painter became more important to him than any school instruction, especially as Laban developed a dialogue with his teacher and acquired life skills as part of the painting lessons. Here was someone from whom the young man could accept criticism. Although he had received acclaim for his paintings from relatives and friends, he could cope with a quite contemptuous response from this man because he regarded him as 'my master'. Nor was this only the admiration of youth. Almost forty years later, when he came to write his autobiographical book *A Life for Dance*, Laban warmly acknowledged that 'through this excellent man, my pastime soon turned into a serious duty and I learned to recognize the value and significance of work'.[8] Above all, the master taught his apprentice how to observe and how to perceive. Almost certainly through this master-painter, Laban was given his introduction to perspective, proportion and the Golden Mean.

At no other time afterward did Laban meet this same strength of challenge or show such deference for anyone's judgement in a particular field of enquiry. For practically the rest of his life, from just before the First World War right through to his death, *he* was the master and everyone looked to *him*. Sometimes his eager students were ready with a challenge but his charisma always dazzled them into submission. Valerie Preston-Dunlop's experience sums up the response of many of those he taught in England:

> I was brim-full of questions about his theories of movement
> from my second year as a student, which were never
> answered . . . eventually the magician in him overwhelmed
> the judgement and I came to believe in him.[9]

The master-painter in Bratislava recognized and nurtured Laban's gift for the visual and plastic arts, though, as yet, movement awareness remained subordinate and closely associated with the pictorial. This was what fashioned and shaped his thinking. He thought, not as a philosopher nor even as a logical theoretician – but as an artist. When he was thinking in tangible, practical terms, his thinking tended to be in picture or narrative form; when he was thinking more abstractly and theoretically his thought was in shape and pattern.

He was the consummate observer. Already as a youngster he had begun discerning formations and patterns and making connections. His painting-master helped him further and he developed the capacity to observe both large and little, both whole and in parts, a capacity he continued to exercise throughout his life.

'He never went anywhere without watching movement,' Lisa Ullmann declared in an interview. 'On a country walk, it might be movement of animals, trees or clouds, but he was especially involved with the movement of people – in trains, in bus stations, in cafés, in classes – he was always thinking about movement and fascinated by the shape and pattern.'[10]

The artist in him enabled him to sketch impressions, see relationships, gain insights. He was an avid note-maker; rarely without pencil and paper, he was perpetually jotting down ideas, observations, symbols, brief records – on all kinds of paper, from the backs of envelopes to the more formal notepad.

He enjoyed thinking but it tended to be entirely visual; making diagrams, sketches, drawings and brief notes rather than coherent sentences connected fluently, one to another. His artistic observation and inclination led him to the three-dimensional, expressive, moving form. He talked about his thinking as 'movement thinking which can be considered as a gathering of impressions in one's mind, for which nomenclature is lacking' (and later as 'impulses which surge and seek an outlet'). He would ponder the patterns and what they might tell us about the human condition.

Laban never had a literary, trained mind. He studied but he seemed to prefer notes and discussion to prolonged reading or writing. He often left others (like Lisa Ullmann) to sort and file his notes. As he himself suggests, it was impressions and impulses that interested him mainly. His thinking remained that of the initiator. He preferred to exhort others to follow through and extend his ideas in detail. Mary Wigman, in her picturesque and persuasive way, underlines this discursive aspect of the man:

> Laban was always a great wanderer who, after entering an unknown country and having found what he wanted, or what happened to meet his need, would soon leave it for

the next one to be explored. But, whenever he stayed, even if it were only for a short time, he left his traces.[11]

True, he thought about and explored areas like notation, space harmony and effort over many years, but seemed less interested in the sustained, ongoing process of arguing an idea to completion. He would observe a pattern and analyse it, grapple for a while with its meaning and then move on. With this tendency to condense and codify rather than expand or elaborate, we find his thinking concentrating either on the basics or on the overall concept.

Though his artist's mind was not interested in logically, philosophically arguing his case, he did feel compelled to communicate his artistic vision in writing. Though he did not feel drawn to test his thesis in any scientific way, he desperately wished to share his discovery of patterns and forms and what they might poetically mean. Above all, he was keen to share his belief in what their significance might contribute to man's understanding of himself and his place in the universe.

Articulating Ideas

Here was a major problem for him. How, with his background and training, could he record his impressions? How could be articulate his findings? The most obvious way was simply to dance them out. This he did for a long time, creating dances and dance-dramas which would say what words could not. But his thinking would not rest there. He was observing patterns that enabled him to come to grips with the very nature of the art. It was not enough for him to choreograph a ballet; he wanted to say what and how it was created. He wanted to clarify the grammar and syntax of movement, to show how other dances could be made, developed and the whole, expressive movement vocabulary extended.

And there was that other stimulus to his thinking. He

knew dance was important, so he was incited to respond whenever he detected others regarding dance as a frivolous, fruitless activity. Always seeking to raise standards and respect for the art, he was spurred on when dance was engaged in by despised professionals or regarded as entertainment for well-meaning amateurs, not really to be taken seriously. Two determinations went hand in hand: one to codify his art and the other to justify it to the world.

First, he needed to overcome the problem of the apparent impermanence of dance and movement. Pictures and sculptures could remain long after the artist had gone. Literature had its written symbols which could give poems, stories and plays some kind of lasting quality. Music had its notation from which others could recreate the musical experience. But dance lasted only for the fleeting moment and then seemed lost for ever.

In order to overcome this, he set himself another twofold task: he believed on the one hand that dance and movement must have its own notation to record it, and so he would have to invent it; and on the other, though he felt it might mean travelling out of his depth, he sought to record *in words* some of his thoughts and findings about the theory which lay behind it.

Writings

It must have taken courage and determination to leap from the world of dance and movement into the world of words. Words were not Laban's natural métier. But he set himself the task of translating from the three-dimensional medium of symbols, shapes and patterns, into the one-dimensional medium of words on the page.

In *The Dancer's World* (1920), Laban clearly recognizes the complexity of his task: to write about an art form where 'conventional language alone is inadequate'. There is as little precedent, he maintains, in dancers writing about dancing as there is of dancers practically exploring new dance activities. He is also fully aware of his own inadequacies as a writer so it is only his determination that enables him to undertake the challenge. If dance is to stand alongside the other arts, and be better understood by a wider public, someone has to attempt the impossible task of writing about it.

He is clear too about what he is not going to do. He is not attempting a rousing discourse nor an instructive lecture nor even a scientific analysis of the dancer's art. Rather, his aim is to awaken insight into, and develop awareness of, the essence of dance and the dancer because of his conviction that dancers can and should assist cultural and creative activity and the understanding of their place in the purpose and destiny of mankind.

And, though he wants to use words, he recognizes that he has to use them in a different manner. He feels the need to find a verbal equivalent of dance form. As a dancer, he must dance 'the dance of his thoughts – in the same way that he carries out the dance of his limbs', creating 'a thought round in which, instead of the visible actions of the moving body, the invisible centres of the thought-processes express their rhythmic play. A dance clothed in words' in which 'the particular trains of thought of the dancer occasionally require to be changed and reformed'.[12] It sounds something akin to a prose poem. He acknowledges that there will be a need for others to expand and where necessary correct (especially in matters scientific or philosophical) his thought rounds to enable his vision to obtain a still wider application.

It will be as well to heed these statements of Laban from the Foreword to his first book, and even regard them as a Foreword applicable to most of his written work. Even those books in English where, because of their layout, we might be led to expect coherent prose, are more easily appreciated when read as a further arrangement of 'thought rounds'.

His lateral thinking naturally finds its way into his writing.

The ideas are not necessarily presented sequentially and rarely is there a chain of reasoning. Often aphoristic, sometimes magpie-like jottings, Laban's approach is fragmentary, regularly indulging in generalizations of a philosophical nature. His writing rarely has the clear logic of standard prose. More often, what he presents is abstract and stylized, indicating shapes, patterns and relationships. There is theme and variation rather than reasoning and proof.

In his dance work, when he was not concerned with shape and pattern, he moved to the dramatic, the narrative, the mythological. These qualities are reflected in his writing. He likes telling a story, but even where it is about his own life, it is not always chronologically ordered nor is it the literal truth. Its truth is more likely to be artistic, conveyed in much the same way as myth and legend.

3 A Language Barrier

With Laban, it was not just a problem of finding a language in which to express the inexpressable, but a problem of which language in which to undertake the task. He was born in Hungary, just 30 miles from Vienna where there were at that time no fewer than five official languages – German, Italian, Bohemian, Polish and Hungarian. With his position in the Austro-Hungarian Army, Laban's father must have been fairly competent in all means of official communication, and the young Rudolf grew up hearing all these languages around him. Not surprisingly, he had a facility for languages in general, but while Hungarian might be said to be his mother tongue, it was not the language he heard most around the home. He could get along in day-to-day parlance in several languages but never achieved a literary mastery of any single one of them.

He never wrote in his native Hungarian – or if he did, nothing of it survives. He had a French governess and his father often spoke in French. From the age of twenty-one to almost thirty, he lived in France. He wrote to Suzanne Perrottet and others in French but most of the material that survives is either in German or (later) in English.

German was the tongue he used most. The majority of his early writing, from the beginning of the 1920s almost to the outbreak of the Second World War, was in German, which was also the language he spoke during that period. So when he began the difficult task of finding words to express dance ideas, he was using the language to which he had grown most accustomed.

His first five books express:

(a) an overview of his ideas about the nature and place of dance (*Die Welt des Tänzers*, 1920)
(b) the values and function of dance in the education of children (*Des Kindes Gymnastik und Tanz*, 1926)
(c) the values and function of dance in the lives of adults (*Gymnastik und Tanz*, 1926)
(d) the principles of form in dance (*Choreographie*, 1926, first part)
(e) an overview of his life as he had attempted to respond to it through dance (*Ein Leben für den Tanz*, 1935).

At this period, we find him for the most part avoiding abstractions, preferring to describe, to comment or philosophize, following the trends of the times.

Between the wars, fashionable German writing reflected a general liking for the romantic, the inspirational, the metaphysical and the philosophical. It was often extravagant language, pictorial, ornate, heavily metaphorical, sentimental and pretentious. At times it was almost kitsch in its expression. So the problems of understanding increase as we not only have to adjust to Laban's patterned thinking and writing but also to the particular use he makes of German. This has proved a nightmare for most translators.

Today, we find much of his German too figurative and folkloric, too mythological and extravagant. His prose often comes over as turgid or effusive. He prefers broad generalizations and expressionistic statements. He finds little interest in developing an idea or illustrating it to give clarity. Rather than illuminating, his writing at times obscures the concepts, leaving the impression of a rather dense text concerned with the eccentric and the mystical. Where we would look for precision and clarification, we find the vague and inexact. This is especially galling when he is employing terminology loosely, always leaving himself the get-out clause that such concepts 'cannot be expressed adequately in words'. We should read his published works in German as essentially the writings of an *artist in his time*. They are not objective, or even analytical works, but subjective attempts to put new thinking about dance on a universal map.

His other main writing is in English, a language in which he took no less interest, but one of which he can be seen to have gained less mastery. He came to England in 1938, having been thinking and writing in German for over twenty years. A year later, that language was the language of the arch enemy, Hitler, and taboo. Laban was sixty years old and faced starting again, not only with his career but also with a new language. To make it worse, he was physically sick and spiritually and morally broken.

As well as still thinking 'in terms of movement' he must also have been 'thinking in terms of German'. Not surprising, then, we find him turning to a much sparser form of expression in English, taking refuge whenever the opportunity arises in the abstract and the geometric.

His five books in English express:

(a) the meaning and economy of effort in industry (*Effort*, 1947)
(b) the value and application of dance in education (*Modern Educational Dance*, 1948)
(c) his movement principles applied to theatre (*Mastery of Movement on the Stage*, 1950)
(d) the principles applied to Kinetographie Laban – his movement and dance notation (*Principles of Dance and Movement Notation*, 1956)
(e) the abstract and mathematical bases of his movement theory (*Choreutics*, 1966).

He worked at his English and built up a large vocabulary but never mastered how to write in it fluently. English for the foreigner has so many complexities of pronunciation, not helped by its archaic spelling; words which sound alike have different meanings (e.g. wood/would), others which sound different have similar meanings (e.g. enough/sufficient). Joan Goodrich indicates the difficulty: Laban was giving a talk at the first summer school in Wales. He had already begun when Joan Goodrich took her place with the other gym teachers in the hall. She began making notes and wrote down, somewhat incredulously, that he seemed to be talking about 'cows'. Then she thought better of it and changed 'cows' to 'cause', though even this alteration left her with the belief that 'I was thoroughly out of my depth.'[13] Later, she discovered that the word he was using was 'chaos' – and while the situation overall may not have been quite that bad, this does illustrate the new language communication problem.

A. Proctor Burman, an engineer and former Olympic skater who worked with Laban in Manchester in 1954, recalled the times, six years earlier, when they had 'worked together on the anglicizing of his unique thoughts and the subjecting of them to a strictly scientific approach'. Burman comments that Laban's 'vocabulary was often more extensive than mine'. It was, however, structuring the words into idiomatic sentences and the 'shades of meaning and often double meanings of our English words' that 'escaped him'. At this stage, Laban was trying to translate those findings he had expressed in German into English, now not just for dancers but for a whole new public in education and industry. And in spite of all their efforts, they were aware that the solutions were not always satisfactory. 'Even now', Burman comments, 'we find that some of the words we chose do not apply equally to both dance and industry'.

Throughout his writing in English, Laban tends to lack the skill and confidence in structuring thought-sequences other than in simple sentences. Rarely does he venture into the complex sentence, and so, although he no longer talks about 'thought rounds', he does tend to place sentences end-to-end instead of weaving them into a continuous line of argument. He remained insecure in his English writing and nearly always required the services of an amanuensis, usually a former student. These enthusiasic individuals,

though competent young English-speakers, could not convey the profundity of Laban's thinking nor live up to his
lifelong experience.

This language barrier echoes another great obstacle in
comprehending Laban, the man and his ideas. In Germany
he worked in dance theatre; in England, with industry. Why
is it so difficult to associate the choreographer with the
industrialist? What is the significance of this great divide?

4   The Broken Line

There seems little connection between Laban's earlier dance work and his later applied-movement activity. When he arrived in England in 1938, he turned his back on dance and choreography and began working in areas removed from the kind of artistic expression which had gained him prestige and renown. It is strange that he should have left behind, literally and metaphorically, everything that he had previously achieved.

Laban was in Berlin during the summer of 1936 where, at fifty-seven, he was the dynamic Director of Dance, at the height of his career, enjoying an international reputation. By the autumn of 1938, he was in Dartington Hall in Devon, a sick, disillusioned refugee of almost sixty years of age. Within a year, the country in which he had arrived was at war with Germany. By September 1939, he must have felt his life, like his success, belonged to the past.

In December 1929, he had celebrated his fiftieth birthday basking in the acclaim of the European dance world. Whole issues of leading dance magazines were devoted to his achievements. In June of the following year, he was at Bayreuth with his dancers and choreographing the 'Bacchanale' in *Tannhäuser* for the Wagner Festival and working alongside Siegfried Wagner and Toscanini. By September, he had a year's contract as ballet-master to the Berlin State Theatres. A year later, this appointment was extended for three more years. In the summer of 1931 he was again in

Bayreuth with a revival of his choreography for the Bacchanale and also managed to continue teaching in Hamburg, Paris and Essen.

In June 1932, his former student, Kurt Jooss, won the International Choreographic Competition in Paris with his ballet *The Green Table*, bringing further honour for Laban as well as a great lift to the status of modern German dance. Though the Berlin State Opera was feeling the financial pinch amidst the Great Depression, it seemed that so many of Laban's long-cherished goals were at last within his reach.

Then, on 30 January 1933, Adolf Hitler was appointed Chancellor and formed his Nazi cabinet. In February, the Reichstag was on fire and on 23 March the enabling law granted Hitler dictatorial powers (until 1937). For quite some time, Laban refused to face it, but all around him things had begun to change for the worse. It remains something of a mystery to this day that a man with such a sense of idealism could brush aside so many signs and indications of the changing circumstances right under his nose.

In September, Dr Goebbels became director of the Reich Chamber of Culture, set up to bring German arts into line with Nazi ideology and collect all creative artists into a unified organization. There were seven sub-chambers covering all aspects of cultural life, each with powers to expel members for 'political unreliability', which meant that anyone seen to be half-hearted about National Socialism could be debarred from practising their art. It took a year or two, but eventually Laban was to feel the effect of this authority.

The persecution of the Jews began almost immediately. In June, one of the principal solo dancers in the Berlin Municipal Opera, Ruth Sorel-Abramovitch, was sacked as a non-Aryan. After the July issue of *Der Tanz*, its general editor, Dr Joseph Lewitan, another non-Aryan, was replaced and before the end of the year Jooss fled the country with his company.

Dr Rudolf Bode, one of Laban's rivals and the champion of German gymnastics, was appointed head of the dance department for the Alliance Fighting for German Culture. Laban's former student, Mary Wigman, and her schools joined the Unit for Body Culture and in writings on dance the emphasis changed to the Germanness of the art, culminating in an article by the respected dance critic, Fritz Boehme, *Is Ballet German?*, in which he argued that dance in Germany should 'rebuke any interference by foreigners'.

The following year Laban was granted German naturalization. His contract with the Berlin State Opera came to an end and a special matinée was arranged in his honour, attended by no less a figure than the Führer himself. Not long after, Laban became Director of the German Dance Theatre under the Ministry of Culture and Propaganda – no doubt each hoped to use the other. Laban ran the German Dance Festival and continued developing courses and showcases for out-of-work dancers with performances at a number of leading Berlin Theatres – all paid for by the Ministry of Propaganda.

The Nazis looked to Laban as an especially useful pawn in the 1936 Olympic Games. The German Dance Festival became the International Dance Festival and it was Laban's task to use his influence to persuade leading figures and companies from around the world to participate. Laban was also appointed head of the Master Dance Workshops designed to train dancers 'for top positions in the profession' and finally to award successful individuals a Master's degree.

Laban had remained in Germany longer than many of his friends and associates felt was either healthy or appropriate. Many artists, scientists and free-thinking intellectuals had either been forced out or chose to leave around 1934. Laban had remained, hoping to continue to further the interests of dance – but he did so at a cost. Wigman (perhaps because she was in a similar position) could see that he had already sacrificed most of his ideals and confided to her diary that Laban was struggling, 'between . . . a wish to survive and what one would call collaboration'.

How can this notion of collaboration possibly be reconciled in such an individual? He was in many ways still an innocent although he had turned fifty. In spite of his military background (or because of it), he remained disinterested, credulous, and at a distance, in matters of politics, always supporting his lack of action with turn-of-the-century fervour because he was 'an artist'. Next to this belief in himself as an artist above the mundane things of life, Laban's ambition was for the art of the dance. The propaganda machine of the Third Reich needed artists and for a while the Nazis not only seemed prepared to tolerate Laban's work but also gave him authority, scope, finance and responsibility for giving dance a place. It was not just a question of survival – how could he turn down the recognition for dance that he had worked a lifetime to achieve?

Amidst some controversy, Laban had been entrusted with the task of creating a vast community dance spectacle involving about one thousand lay-dancers from all over Germany, in the arts festival alongside the 1936 Olympic Games. Here was the chance to show not just Germany but the whole world some of his ideas and methods. He began planning and rehearsing a piece called *From the Warm Wind and the New Joy*, with a text from Nietzsche's *Thus Spake Zarathustra*. It was to be presented just before the opening of the official Games, in the brand-new, Greek-style auditorium, the Dietrich Eckart Theatre at the south-west corner of the Olympic site. Towards the end of June, a dress-rehearsal was held which Goebbels, the Minister of Propaganda, attended. He stayed fifteen minutes and left. Later, in his diary, Goebbels declared, 'it is dressed up in our clothes and has nothing to do with us'. It seems he did not care for the freedom of expression that Laban's movements gave to the individual. But whatever his reasons, Goebbels banned the actual performance from the Festival and, from that point on, Laban's position rapidly declined.

The International Dance Festival took place in July, but Laban had not been able to engage many of the top companies or personalities from abroad. The festival was intended to be equal in stature to the Olympic Games, so it was planned as a competition. But when Laban was instructed that a German company must win, he, with characteristic cunning, side-stepped the issue by giving everyone an honorary certificate of participation.

It was also originally intended that Laban should collaborate with Hans Niedecken-Gebhardt for the grand opening event to take place on the evening of 1 August in the main Olympic Stadium. The fourth scene was dedicated to dance with heroic fight and lament. Wigman performed the climactic scene with 80 dancers but by the time it all came to fruition, Laban's place in the organization had been taken over and he was suddenly under suspicion.

Laban became ill and went to Plauen to try to recover but the authorities continued to investigate him and his background. Early in 1937 he was under 'house arrest' in an uninhabited monastery in Schloss Banz, where he made a last-minute attempt to write positively about the future of German dance. But it all proved useless. There was a campaign against him in the press. His work was banned by Hitler and Laban's name was forbidden to be used anywhere in the Third Reich. It was clear to his friends that under the present regime Laban's forward-looking theory and practice had no future and the only chance of personal survival now was for him to leave Germany. By November, on the pretext of an invitation to speak at the Sorbonne, Laban left for Paris, hoping to find his former associate Dussia Bereska.

By this time, the exiled Ballet Jooss company had been invited by the Elmhirsts to make their permanent home at Dartington Hall in England.* Early in 1938, Kurt Jooss heard of Laban's sickness in Paris and went to visit him. Jooss was so concerned when he witnessed Laban's state of illness and distress that he eventually persuaded him to travel to the UK to be his guest at Dartington. On 6 February 1938, a depressed, downcast, ailing Rudolf Laban arrived in Devon. Here, the great champion of the new dance, who had struggled for a lifetime to bring it status, confided to Jooss that, 'I care little whether I see a moving, dancing body ever again.'[14]

Apart from his disillusionment, it would have seemed inappropriate to have spoken about his work in Germany, let alone to have broached anything about Hitler and his initial support for dance. In any case, in wartime Britain, there was little room for the New Dance, especially, as it was then, the New German Dance. The world of traditional classical ballet in Britain – as elsewhere – was resistant to his ideas and influences, in spite of the successful tours of the Ballet Jooss. So, all Laban could do was either give up, or seek other opportunities.

For a while, he might well have wanted to give up but for a young ballet teacher from the Ballet Jooss School, Lisa Ullmann. It was she who over those first months in England visited him and gradually, though it took some years, nurtured him back to full activity in what looked like, and has tended to remain, a separate and separated series of activities.

In spite of incredible odds, he did bounce back. But not in

---

* Leonard and Dorothy Elmhirst established contact with Jooss in 1933 in their role as the founders of the Dartington Hall Trust. In April 1934, Sigurd Leeder, some of the staff, and 22 students of the Folkwangschule left Germany to join Jooss at Dartington and the Jooss–Leeder School was established. It was the first professional activity of the newly formed Arts Department administered by Christopher Martin.

the old style, no longer the champion of the dance. Fresh footholds allowed him to start all over again, building new reputations and stimulating the application of his work to some areas that previously had only been touched on in his theory and practice.

He found new students and delighted in talking about his ideas. He would reminisce about his childhood and early pioneering days in Ascona, but the dance in Germany he preferred to forget. Those last few years under the Nazis especially seemed to remain something of a nightmare that he could never bear to recall. Certainly he never talked or wrote about them and though after the Second World War he returned to the continent to visit old friends and acquaintances, he never set foot in Germany again. By that stage he may have had a more objective view of those years with the Third Reich. It all remained too painful for him to want to relive his disappointment with what he had, and what he had not quite, achieved for the art of the dance.

Right through to the point of his death, all his great dance pioneering remained behind a veil. It is only now that we can begin to work on the jigsaw and find those connections that once again allow us to consider his work as a whole.

Part Two
LABAN'S IDEAS IN CONTEXT

'... I think what captivated his imagination was the possibility of encompassing the whole width of artistic development by a single child of his brain – the human body's movement.'

Dr Joseph Lewitan, founder of the magazine *Der Tanz*

5   Practical Experiences

Self-made Man?

Many individuals who develop theories trace their influences
to academic sources, to reading, to forerunners in the field
of enquiry. Not so with Laban. 'I did not find the basis of
my insights in the works of the intellectual giants,' he
declares towards the end of *The Dancer's World*. 'My
knowledge comes exclusively from the dance itself: the
exchange of ideas with hundreds of living, enthusiastic
dancers, together with my practical experience as an artist,
dancing teacher and director.' More telling for him than
reading, then, are the influences of his background and
practical experience and the people he worked with. By
1951, as he looked back, he was identifying the impetus
which led him to study movement and dance not as a single
force but 'a string of events which drive you along the way of
destiny'.[1]

Young Onlooker

This string of events began early. Laban's father's postings
took him far away from his son, to Turkey; and, out of duty,
his mother followed her husband to attend to the social
activity which surrounded the Governorship of Bosnia-
Herzegovina. Laban remained at home in Pressburg, left to
his own devices. As often happens when young people are
surrounded by adults who have little time for them as
children, or are left on their own a great deal, the 'aloneness'

establishes in the individual a keen and shrewd observation of surrounding events and a capacity to absorb them.

For some, it is a language absorption; for others, music becomes part of their being. In Laban's case, he was surrounded by and involved in movement, and it was this that most drove him 'along the way of destiny'. Most boys like activity, but from early days he was aware of that physicality. He is not so special in having a vivid imagination, but he expressed his imagination regularly in physical images and movement activity.

The family home bordered the Danube. Across the bridge was forested countryside where he would play alone and fantasize, turning the long-legged birds into witches and the squirrels into gnomes and goblins from whom he would playfully escape. Additionally, there was the movement of travel. Wherever he or the family journeyed, there were new domains to conquer and even the inanimate images stirred his imagination. Waves 'danced' for him; fishes 'leapt'; stones 'sparkled' as they became the treasury before the caves belonging to mountain kings, and the mountains themselves were huge monsters to be physically encountered.

So vivid and kinetic were these childhood experiences that they could be recalled and relived almost 40 years later when he came to write *A Life for Dance*. 'Mountains were giants', he wrote, and then remarkably but effortlessly transfers the narrative into the present: 'Now, as then, I can feel how I climb along the flank of one. I scramble up his ragged chest, clutching at each hair to pull me up'. And for almost two pages he re-experiences childhood events which brought him in such close physical proximity with nature that he could talk of 'the earth my confidante . . . the mistress of giants and elves, wood sprites and water nymphs'[2] of whom he could ask questions that he had been unable to ask anyone else.

Though still a schoolboy, he is not just active and

imaginative – taking his clothes off and stretching his arms to the blue sky – but most unusually, we find him relating the two and speculating about the meaning and universality of it all. 'Heaven and earth are mother and father of man, I thought, and I rejoiced to be a human being and jubilantly raced the rapid brooks down into the valley.'

Creating Theatre

Laban heard stories from relations and friends, some fiction, some built upon fact about other relatives or their childhood days. These were turned by the young Rudolf into other fantasies which were then given physical, three-dimensional expression in plays for his Kasperl, a version of Punch and Judy puppet theatre.

Even these plays were symbolic, acting out and making one kind of sense of the people, the events and the world around him. Other experiences were turned into melodrama. Physical events like breaking school windows, being expelled, running away from home, he turned into one-man ballads which he again performed alone.

Freedom and Discipline

During the little time he did spend at school, he seems to have occupied some of his energies in devising how to avoid it. Even in gymnastics, he was sensing an objection to its formality and limited range. On one occasion, when told to climb the ropes, he swung his way out through an open window and ran off to the nearby woods. There he waited for the other boys from his dancing troupe. He was no more than thirteen when he first founded and became the leader of the czárdás for a Budapest Youth Group.

As he grew a little older, his awareness became broader and he began to observe not just people moving but the quality of their movement. Pressburg (Bratislava, in what

was then southern Bohemia in Hungary), was a centre
bordering on a number of other countries. It was the late
nineteenth century and gradually even in this small town the
industrial revolution was infiltrating the largely rural life.

Work and Recreation

Laban began noticing movement differences between people
working without machines and those working with them. He
was also intrigued by the way people used their energies in
work and recovered them through play which he saw was, at
its best, literally re-creation.

One of the surest forms of revitalization of the human
spirit, he noticed, was dance. He observed dancing at
weddings, dancing at funerals and folk dancing from all over
the Austro-Hungarian Empire – by Hungarians, Turks,
Czechs and Russians. 'When I was a child,' he remembered
in a *News Sheet* article in 1951, 'peasant dances, religious
processions, court ceremonials and similar movement manifestations, were still alive in my home country. They were
not only alive, but an integral part of social existence. If one
grows up surrounded by people to whom forceful and gay,
solemn and deeply felt leisure time activity is an important
part of life, one cannot fail to be impressed by the richness of
such events.'[3] But unhappily, that definite link between
work, worship and leisure where each employed rhythm,
song and lively movement, began to disappear.

Work that previously had involved good bodily carriage
and free, open movement, was beginning to be replaced by
steam and steel. For the young Laban who, even in his early
teens, remarkably registered all this, the contrast became
symbolized in the replacing of the old-time floating boat
bridge by a modern suspension bridge.

'I remember,' he continued in *A Life for Dance*, 'when the
gaily painted boat bridge over the half-mile-wide Danube
was open for the passage of barges full of chanting peasant

folk on a pilgrimage, still more colourful than the bridge. And the men who rowed beside the boats constituting the passage-gap sang also and had laughing vigorous faces. Then a huge steel and concrete suspension bridge was built and the flowery boat bridge disappeared and pilgrims took the dirty train over the new bridge.'

Escape to Theatre

From the age of fourteen, because one of his uncles was a kind of custodian for the local theatre, he had easy access to ballet, opera and drama, both backstage and from the auditorium, at the Municipal Opera House in Pressburg. Its activity and atmosphere clearly impressed him. By the time he was seventeen, he was assisting with the design and execution of décor and costumes as well as acting as an unpaid assistant stage manager. His big chance came when the history of the town was to be presented on the state occasion of the emperor's visit to the region.

Left to his own devices to organize friends and relatives into tableaux, he discovered how much more interesting they could be if the participant moved from one position to another and the tableaux were interspersed with folk dances and performed to the accompaniment of music. This was the beginning of a long association with festival and pageant, and their contribution to the rhythm of effort and recovery.

Young Choreographer

Experiences of this sort gave him the confidence to arrange the dances for the final festival of the military cadets. He had set out with rather grandiose ideas but eventually realized that one of the best ways of celebrating the occasion was to use just what the hundred men from all over the Austro-Hungarian Empire had to offer by way of native skill and tradition. He was in his element not only organizing waltzes, czárdás, line and circle dances, mazurkas, polkas, landlers, Schuhplattlers, tarantellas and various other peasant dances, but auditioning groups and individuals before teaching them and structuring the entire entertainment. What an opportunity, what an influence on a twenty-year-old individual interested in dance to come into such close contact with such a wide range of ethnic expression.

Dervish Dancers

Whenever Laban was recalling major events of his life, he would include the visits he made to the monasteries of the dervishes, where he witnessed their dancing as genuine acts of worship. 'Great impression – the dancing of the Dervishes', he notes in the biographical outline for *Schrifttanz* in 1927. Unlike most of the other events influencing his movement destiny, this one had the additional opportunity of conversation and instruction.

Throughout his journeying in Turkey, when he was visiting his father in Bosnia-Herzegovina, he was placed under the protection of the imam who lived in a nearby village. Amongst the Mohammedan inhabitants of that village was a sheikh and a group of Mevlevi. Laban soon made friends with the sheikh and often rode over to talk with him. It was these conversations which led him to be introduced to the secret ceremonies of the dervishes.

No wonder Laban found them fascinating, for here were a group of Muslim lay-monks who did not say their prayers in words but danced them in endless circling, turning movements. Dervish dancers begin their whirling movements slowly and stately, holding out their arms with one hand up, to symbolize the reception of divine grace, and pointing down to pass on the divine grace to others. The steps move them around the area while the dancers themselves turn in a circle, a circle that represents the orbit of the planets. By this praying with the body, they reached their ecstasy and experienced an unspoken link with the infinite. Nevertheless, young Laban was not at first convinced. 'Dances of the Dervishes are to us, at first sight, incomprehensible. They are almost repulsive', he comments in *A Life for Dance*. 'The dancers turn until they froth at the mouth . . . That wise men with long beards gave themselves completely to this and even insisted it was in the service of God, seemed peculiar to me.'

Then, one day, he saw the full effect that the trance could have over the body and its function and he began to consider a deeper significance.

> I saw to my astonishment, how these Dervishes, in the state of highest ecstasy, pushed needles and nails through their cheeks, chests and arms without any sign of pain, and what's more, without any trace of blood. Afterwards, there was no wound to be seen; the muscles closed immediately. When they started using sharp knives on themselves, I recalled the belief of the old mountain farmer who maintained that through the magic of the dance, a body can be made 'knife-safe'.[4]

He returned again and again to these images. 'Wasn't there something great, something considerable behind it all? Could the Dervishes really have made themselves immune to cuts? Could dancing really have such an effect upon man?' Later, it led him to think about movement and the control of the circulation of the blood, about circle and round dances and their place in a universal view of existence. He retained a belief that dance could be an expanding activity for everyone, linking the individual space to infinite space.

In a newspaper article in 1921, Mary Wigman records,

> To experience the dance and to produce it not only became Laban's personal task, but he also felt it was, the task of all dancers, the ethical basis of dance teaching, the cosmic experience, religion.

Fertile Ground

Even though, by the time he reached twenty-one years of age, Laban found himself unable to set off on his chosen career with clarity (he was to spend some seven more years away from full-time dance), that destiny he spoke of had already shown his predilections and established dexterities, attitudes, patterns in the way he was to go. He had discovered the joy of physical expression, had started exploring ways of reshaping experience for communication to others. He had proved himself a dreamer but one with considerable design and organizing ability. Fascinated by the world around him, especially its three-dimensionality in the colour, shape, quality, form of its movement, his early experiences set up insights and foundations on which he continued to build throughout his life.

He had begun exercising his movement observation, his movement memory and his movement imagination. Already, his externally disciplined spirit in perpetually seeking freedom of expression was seeking also to understand tension and relaxation and how they might be harnessed in the natural rhythm of things. He had seen that while it was possible to believe in the influence of 'mind over matter', it was every bit as important to recognize the influence of 'matter over mind'.

He had also begun employing the most reflective part of his nature as he pondered not just the shape, formation and power of movement but what they might mean in and for the life of man and his relationship with the universe. He was aware of a dissatisfaction with the way things are and a belief that greater understanding could lead to richer experience in the art of living.

6 Theoretical Foundations

In spite of his protestations, Laban's experience can be seen to relate to ideas that were already current. There are existing foundations on which he might have built and shaped his own ideas. Though in *The Dancer's World* Laban insisted he had not drawn on the works of intellectuals, he does provide a reading list which includes texts on dancing, anatomy, notation, physiology and psychology, but points out that 'as purely rational works do not contribute to a clear and distinct appreciation of the dance', those works which are included 'have arisen from a more comprehensive view of the world'[5] and so eliminate ideas touched upon in his book. In *A Life for Dance*, which is the nearest Laban gets to biography, he does not refer to a single article nor does he mention the influence of any book.

In all kinds of ways, some tangible, some less so, ideas are gathered and scattered. We take over concepts and attitudes all our lives without necessarily acknowledging or even knowing from whence they came. This is applicable both to Laban's use of the concepts of others and the use other people have made of Laban's ideas. A good deal of Laban's work and theory has become so basic and forms the foundation of so much of our understanding of movement, that quite often people come to regard it now as common belief.

It is hardly possible, when considering an active, developing mind, to point out accurately from whom it took this or that idea, or who helped it develop a particular notion. It is already clear that Laban was not a scholar in the conventional sense, and certainly not an avid reader. He seems generally to have preferred to learn about the ideas of others through conversation and discussion. There are, however, books and practitioners with which he certainly had some affinity or from whom he appears to have derived impressions and impulses.

Speculation could lead into all kinds of claims, so selection needs to be confined to those works which evidence from Laban himself or his colleagues clearly suggests had a bearing on his thinking process at crucial points of his developing theory. This can then be checked by further examination of the writings of those key thinkers and pioneers to identify areas of correspondence.

Plato and the Platonic

Laban was drawn to Greek thinking. He enjoyed Greek roots and word formations. From the classic background he devised new terms such as 'choreosophie' and 'choreology', and brought words like 'kinetic' into more regular use and awareness. He makes passing reference to Aristotle, Pythagoras, Plato and several times refers to Lucian and his awareness of the power of dance, especially without music. Several of those close to him even spoke of him as a Platonist. Jooss talks authoritatively of Laban's interest in Plato's ideas, especially as outlined in the *Timaeus*.

Plato was an Athenian, born around 427 BC. As a young man, he met Socrates and this influence turned him from his interest in writing poetry to an approach to philosophy which contains elements of both the moral and the metaphysical. The *Timaeus* is a work of Plato's later years and stands as a landmark in the history of European thought. It is written in the form of a sequel to the *Republic*. In the dialogue, Timaeus, a Pythagorean philosopher, presents an exposition of the origin and system of the universe. Its prime focus is on certain philosophical principles, on aspects of astronomy, on the structure of matter, on human psychology and physiology, all of which areas had been of prime importance to Laban throughout his life.

Plato's concepts, however, like those of Laban, are often difficult to determine with absolute accuracy though broad lines of argument emerge which would have interested Laban. With both of them, we are often in a world of metaphor where we seek philosophic meaning. Often in Plato, concepts emerge which come close to coinciding with attitudes and concepts which Laban himself promulgated.

In the *Timaeus* there is concern for the design and purpose of things in the material world. Plato recognizes a power behind the cosmos and a divine purpose mentioning the creator in a number of metaphors but indicating that the creator/gods have an overall plan and purpose and created the stars, animals and man according to certain geometrical formulae. Plato follows the existing idea in Greek thought that the orbit of heavenly bodies has a place in the divine design and goes on to declare that there is a link between the structure and behaviour of the whole world (the macrocosm) and that of man (the microcosm).

The construction of the heavens is spoken of in terms of rings, often set one within another at an angle. Plato traces the origins of sensations and diseases, and briefly indicates man's fate after death. Throughout Laban's writing, there is an underlying belief in an ultimate harmonious structure of the universe.

In a paper published in 1959 (the year after his death), Laban postulates elements of the harmonious universal structure seeing links between orbiting planets, cell structures and life. There is a correspondence between the part and the whole, whether it be universal states or the human body.

All the possible virtues and volitions exist and are fulfilled in an exemplary way, in the life of the cells. We could, of course, suppose that these noble tendencies are infiltrated from above – that is, the cells learn their pride, modesty, their capacity to be social and energetic from the examples set and advice given from the governing cell group. But, alas, this illusion is revealed by the fact that the most anti-social mind often enjoys the most wonderful harmonious and smoothly functioning cell life. Is it not more true that the anti-social governing cell groups of a healthy and harmonious cell state, have failed to learn from their subordinates to distinguish right from wrong?"[6]

The creator, for Plato, is a craftsman who determined to make a moving image of eternity. His plan includes a complex system of Forms which have subordinate and related Forms. Form is the first of the three factors in the universe identified by Plato. The second resembles or 'copies' it but 'is in constant motion', and is apprehended by the means of sensation. Finally, Plato identifies space, which provides a position for everything that comes to be'. Here Laban could find other points of departure. Shapes in space and the shapes which make up the elements were amongst those which intrigued him most. Studies in crystallography and mathematics, enquiring into the structure of the atom and the crystal, kept Laban fascinated all his life and looking for the evidence that would link the shape of the crystal with the shape into which he placed the human form and its movement.

Of special interest in Plato's scheme of things is his attempt to apply mathematics to nature even though he does not distinguish between the geometric shape and the material particle. He attempts to account for differences between and transformations of different types of matter in terms of mathematical patterns. Building on Pythagorean philosophy, Plato identifies 'four types of perfect body'. Geometrically, solids (inorganic life) are bounded by planes and the most elementary, fundamental plane figure is the triangle. Two types of triangle are recognized and four basic solids are constructed from them.

Equilateral triangles form the rectangle and triangles with

60- and 30-degree angles form the octahedron, the pyramid and the icosahedron. In *Choreutics*, Laban maintains that 'Pythagoras proved that the human body is built according to the Golden Section.'[7]

After much trial and error, Laban decided that the icosahedron was the figure within which the human body could best express space relationships and the tensions which all parts of the body can project. By seeing the body in the icosahedron, Laban felt that he was pointing to the link, the relationship between human anatomy, cell structure and the whole cosmos.

Plato discusses the concept of Time and the measurement of time especially in relation to the heavens with which it came into being, raising the further question of the nature of the force which causes the movement of the heavenly bodies. Plato's dynamics were operative in a system that could be understood so that the force underlying the universe must be part of the overall design. Laban echoes this in his statement that all movement is purposeful, has a cause and a function. Plato held that bodies in motion must either be in motion driven by another force or have the source of motion within themselves and here again Laban picks up the idea in distinguishing between what he at one point refers to as 'motion' of the inanimate and 'movement' of the animate.

Again, Plato's observation that the only things capable of motion without some external impetus are things that have life, certainly underpins Laban's view that the quality of movement in a living thing (its nature and function) is an indication of the quality of life.

In the *Republic*, Plato talks of the three parts of the mind (soul), though he leaves out areas of human experience such as perception and sensation. In the *Timaeus*, the three parts are located in different parts of the body: the head holds the powers of reasoning and decision-making (he does not distinguish the will as separate). He sees them as the immortal part of the soul but they are linked to the mortal parts in the rest of the body.

The two other parts are linked, with the heart where are located the feelings and emotions, and the gut or abdomen, where the more physical appetites are situated. While his lack of understanding of the nervous system is something of a handicap, his ideas do stress the close relationship between mind and body and the way in which the one affects the other – all ideas which Laban incorporated to some degree in his own work.

Plato distinguishes between the truths of logic and mathematics and those derived from general experience. Laban is more likely to emphasize the truth found in experience and insists that it is a mistake to look to intellectual works to discover the foundations of modern dance experience.

Laban may well have taken a lead from Plato but does not seem to have made any detailed or thorough study of him. He talked about the ideas of Plato to fellow workers, but does not himself attempt to be scientific in his approach.

Whenever he first came across Platonic ideas, it is unlikely that Laban met them as early as his schooldays, since he saw so little of the classroom during that period. It is more likely that he met the mathematics of Pythagoras while he was apprenticed to the local painter in Pressburg. Every good art student has a grounding in Pythagoras, especially in relation to the Golden Section.

As early as 1924, Gertrud Snell, whom Laban discovered had a keen interest in mathematics, had worked with him on aspects of human movement in relation to the icosahedron and had assisted him in developing the scales, but she did not show much interest in Plato.

Many of the sketches and drawings Laban completed between the wars show bodies moving in triangular and similar mathematical forms. By the time he reached England, he seemed again to be enjoying the mathematical shapes and spent much time while at Dartington simply building models based on the Pythagorean solids in what Jooss referred to as his sorcerer's cave. By that point Laban was delighting in the aesthetic quality of his crystalline model even more than in their philosophical or mathematical importance.

Jean-Georges Noverre

Amongst the few books from Laban's between-the-wars bookshelf that have survived is a copy of a first edition of Noverre's *Lettres sur La Danse, Le Ballet et Les Arts*. This 1803 revised and enlarged four-volume quarto edition contains Noverre's letters on the dance, together with his correspondence with Voltaire, a number of letters on the fine arts in general and the scenarii of a number of his ballets. It was published by Schnoor at St Petersburg and was one of the most cherished items Laban owned. It is this edition that he lists amongst the recommended reading at the end of *The World of the Dancer*.

He was not a person who cared much about possessions but ever since he had been studying in Paris, Laban had regarded Noverre's ideas highly. Maja, his second wife, soon became well aware of his interest and, though she was bringing up their young family and could ill afford it, sacrificed a great deal in order to make the Noverre publication her special present to her husband.

Like Laban, Noverre had a father in the army (serving under Charles XII) who wanted his son to take up a military career. Born in Paris in 1727, Noverre came from a different tradition, however, and seems to have found support from his parents for his interest in the theatre. After a good general education, he was given the opportunity to become the pupil of Louis Dupré, a celebrated dancer of the time. He was still only sixteen by the time he had put in an appearance at the Opéra-Comique. He then accepted an invitation to join a company appearing at the court of Frederick the Great but became dissatisfied when he found the treatment he received was more appropriate for soldiers than for artists.

Back in France, and after protracted negotiations, he finally signed a contract to go to London as part of Garrick's Drury Lane season in the winter of 1755. The *Lettres* were probably written while Noverre was in England. Noverre and his company had not proved a success even though Garrick saw in him 'the Shakespeare of the Dance'. But on his return to France, Noverre wanted to share with his countrymen the new concept of the ballet which Garrick's acting had stimulated him into formulating and the *Lettres sur La Danse* were published simultaneously in Lyons and Stuttgart in 1760.

Noverre's *Lettres* are an exposition of the theories of dance and the laws underpinning its representation. They argue for a return to principles based on nature and the natural and in their observations of practice then current are a kind of contemporary history of the dance at that point and stand unrivalled in the influence that they have exerted on ballet ever since. According to Horst Koegler, both Fokine and Laban referred to Noverre as their model.[8]

Noverre was an innovator and proceeded to use his considerable knowledge of and experience in choreography to reform all aspects of his profession. He chooses to face up to all manner of questions pertaining to dance through a series of letters answering imaginary questions put to him. Noverre sets out his criticisms of the qualities, both good and bad, of many of the great dancers of his time and in so doing fills in fascinating details of the ballets, their costumes and production styles.

Things had not changed a great deal in 140 years between Noverre writing and Laban reading, and Laban could warm to the attack on the artificiality and frivolity of the dance. Though masks were no longer worn during Laban's day, costume was still exaggerated and toes artificially turned out. Noverre called for a return to a more natural approach based on painting and drawing, where less attention was paid to symmetry and more to variety. He wanted a closer relationship between movement, music, action and design, leading to a ballet which had an overall shape and structure. He pleads that ballets should be an integrated part of any stage presentation, actively developing the theme and not regarded as mere divertissements showing clever physical skill. True, physical skill was important for Noverre but he maintained that without feeling and expression, the dance would not move the human spirit. The choreography of the new ballet should focus more on character and situation.

He called for good music, appropriate costume and above all purposeful content unfolded through a sound plot. Ballets should be consistent and serious, dance-dramas with subjects more akin to tragedy than frolic.

Though his *Lettres* were much acclaimed during his lifetime, they also stirred a great deal of indignation and abuse from dancers and others who were entrenched in their ways or pretentious in their outlook. Many found his reforming ideas too much and maintained that he was attacking their great traditions and ancient principles. He remains, however, one of the most intelligent and articulate men in the history of dance.

In the *Lettres*, Laban had seen a kindred spirit and one who had expressed many of those attitudes towards the dance that he had increasingly voiced from his early experience of dance at the local theatre in Pressburg, deploring those performances in which the showy and the merely virtuoso became so intrusive. Laban was to spend his next 30 years exploring and putting into practice those attitudes and his own feeling for the dramatic in dance on stages, platforms and open spaces throughout Europe and the near East.

François Delsarte

Though he never mentioned him in print, Laban did acknowledge the stimulus that he received from the ideas of François Delsarte. Lisa Ullmann believed that while in Paris during the period 1900 to 1908, Laban had met a former friend or pupil of Delsarte and learnt something of the approach from him. Early biographical outlines include entries from the 1900–8 era such as 'studied ballet and Delsarte mime'.

Some 30 years earlier, in 1871, Delsarte had died in Paris. He had been born 60 years before that in Solesmes, the first of two male children. Several versions of his early life exist, but all agree that he arrived in Paris at an early age. When he was only six years old, his father died a bankrupt, and his mother, in order to obtain work to bring up the children, went to live in Paris. Within a few years, however, both his mother and his younger brother also died, leaving François alone and destitute. He was already noticeable for his musical gifts and fortunately, before long, Delsarte obtained a scholarship to study singing and acting at the Conservatoire.

As a result of some thoroughly bad teaching, however, Delsarte's voice was ruined and so he had to abandon any ideas of a singing or acting career. But the experience set him thinking and researching into the very fundamentals of expresssion. His own teachers had limited themselves to a stylized, arbitrary and artificial approach, showing no understanding of basic principles involved in body and voice work.

Delsarte's quest returned him to a search for the natural depiction of feeling in both body and voice. He devoted the rest of his life to discovering what laws could be said to underlie human expression – especially in gesture and mime and to finding ways of freeing the natural voice and movement.

He believed that all arts and sciences had a trinitarian basis – he divided the body into three zones of head, torso and limbs and held that all three were inseparable in human expression and balance. Through his 'law of correspondence', he emphasized the interdependency throughout man's being, pointing out that the spiritual side of man affects the physical and the physical affects the spiritual.

Delsarte maintained that the trunk was central (both in position and concept), the head was the means by which control was exercised and the limbs were the freest, most mobile part of man's existence. The fundamental principle of expression, he said, was strength and control at the centre, with freedom at the extremities.

His understanding of gesture is based on his division of the human existence into the intellect, the feeling and the physical, channelled by the triple division of the natural laws of time, motion and space. His 'system' has nine laws of gesture and posture, on which he based his exercises for freedom and relaxation – intending to educate each part of the body to express emotions and ideas intelligibly.

He set about his investigations with thoroughness. His example may have spurred Laban in his own studies. He undertook a complete anatomy course at medical school in order to understand the physiology of the human body. Delsarte spent a great deal of his time in observing how people react through voice and movement at times of great emotion. He looked at children at play, adults at work, at people in moments of great joy and excitement and at others in moments of sorrow and disaster. He observed the self-assured, the depressed, the rich, the poor and folk with all sorts of temperaments, problems and diseases.

Delsarte was also interested in the harmony of things and formulated a number of associations and relationships which must have proved interesting to Laban. He analysed gestures and expressions of the body, and divided the movement into three categories which he termed excentric, concentric and normal, referring to movement at the centre (normal), going out from the centre (excentric) and going towards the centre (concentric). Every movement, he pointed out, had tensions, relaxation, balance and form and consists of:

motion   space   time
force   form   design.

Emphasizing the importance of recognizing man as physical (vitality and life), emotional (conduct and relationships) and mental (thought and intellect), he says:

> For the expression of this triune nature, man has three languages, the word, the tone and the gesture.[9]

His observations led him to argue that the physical side of man's nature comes first, since we begin to experience through sensations. Then comes the moral development, through feeling and emotion, and finally thought and ideas, which are the mental. In childhood, sensations are first developed through voice and its tones, then with the need to express emotion, likes and dislikes, the child explores gesture. Finally, with development of thought and idea comes the ever-increasing use of words. Delsarte anticipated Laban in pointing out that once man has acquired the use of words, there is a tendency for him to neglect his skill in gesture and tone. With time, his speech becomes more articulate, his body less so.

Similarly with regard to the effects of a more urban and industrialized society, Delsarte, like Laban, saw growing stress and tension building in certain parts of the body, preventing the whole person from enjoying its flow and flexibility. So Delsarte became concerned with the means of relaxation to overcome unnecessary muscular tension. His aim was to train the body until as a matter of habit, unconsciously, it remained flexible. By establishing a natural state free of nervous tension, the body could move from discord to harmony and, instead of being self-conscious, it became self-possessed for expression through movement. Within a few years of his leaving Paris, at one of his Monte

Verità schools, Laban was advertising a course to study 'Dance, Tone, Word and Form'.

Delsarte made use of all the knowledge he had acquired in courses and lectures he gave, maintaining that the basic principles which governed what he called 'applied aesthetics' were applicable to all the art forms whether musical (instrumental or vocal), histrionic (acting or oratorical), or fine art (plastic or graphic). Famous artists of every persuasion and from all parts of the world visited him and went away enthusiastic about his ideas.

By the time Delsarte died in Paris 1871, he had formulated a number of what he regarded as the laws of expression but had not committed anything to print. Most of what does survive is in the form of charts and somewhat enigmatic jottings; like Laban after him, he held that his theory was still evolving and incomplete. Illness in the later years of his life meant that he found it harder to promulgate his ideas through his lectures and demonstrations and his influence might have faded had it not been for a few individuals who recognized the lasting value of many of his ideas and went on teaching them to others.

From the United States, the actor Steele MacKaye went to visit Delsarte in Paris and stayed to study with him for eight months during the two years before his death. Without MacKaye, Delsarte's ideas may have fallen out of fashion sooner (certainly in the States) but MacKaye popularized the *System of Oratory* through his 'Harmonic Gymnastics'.

This and other factors brought about a revival of interest in Delsarte teaching around the turn of the century. In Paris, by the time Laban was there, Delsarte still had a number of followers and it seems likely that in the dance and performance circles that Laban frequented there were a number of devotees of the Delsarte system with whom he could discourse. (Later, in 1954, Ted Shawn wrote a book about the man and his work, *Every Little Movement*. 'Through his body, man gives form to feeling.')

Emil Jaques-Dalcroze

Though apparently Laban and Dalcroze met but briefly and, no doubt, Laban would not wish to acknowledge any direct influence from Dalcroze, there are too many close associations to allow anyone studying Laban to ignore some definite acquaintance with the ideas of Emil Jaques-Dalcroze.

Another teacher of music (Walter Sorrell claims he was also a Platonist and it certainly appears he was aware of the work of Delsarte), Dalcroze exercised considerable influence in the world of dance. He was born in 1865, in Vienna (not many miles along the Danube from where Laban himself was born), of Swiss Romansche stock and spent most of his life in Geneva. In 1892 he became a professor at the Conservatoire, teaching theory and harmony. As a composer, he enjoyed some success in Switzerland with his five operas which were regularly performed. As a professor, he grew more and more dissatisfied with the results of his teaching.

Being a thoughtful and conscientious individual, he began puzzling about the difficulties encountered by his students in sustaining rhythm. His own training had been in the 'classical' mode, highly disciplined, strongly intellectual and rigid in its approach. He soon realized that something very different was needed.

A wave of renewed interest in the Greeks was apparent. During the early part of the century Isadora Duncan toured Europe with her version of the revived classic Greek dance. Dalcroze himself looked to the Greek ideal especially in the harmony of soul and body and began to look for ways to release the natural rhythm within the individual. At first he had sought to train the hearing potential alone, but soon realized that some students still encountered problems in measuring and above all responding to time measures and rhythmic values. This led him to seek to enable students to respond with their bodies to music and invented exercises involving walking, stopping, turning, etc. with the sound, always holding in mind the need to keep the response as natural as possible. This was the origin of his 'good rhythm' – Eurhythmics.

Soon he began to expand his approach until every rhythmic detail of a composition would be expressed through the movement of the body. From this, he proceeded to visualization, sometimes of an entire symphonic work, with each 'dancer' following a specific instrument, phrase for phrase. Opposition from the traditionalists at the Academy drove him to hire a hall and set up on his own.

He too extended his understanding by enlisting the help of a physiologist (Professor Matthis Lussy) who explored the relationship between musical movement in time and bodily movement in space. Dalcroze asked the psychologist, Professor Edouard Claperède to help him formulate a basis for his belief in the relationship between 'the discipline of emotion and the practice in reaction'.

One evening in the spring of 1906, Dalcroze gave one of his lecture/demonstrations in Geneva. In the auditorium was the theatre designer Adolphe Appia who found the experience a revelation. At last he felt he had discovered the way 'to reform the art of the theatre' and to bring into closer contact the music and the performer. 'I found the answer to my passionate desire for synthesis,' Appia wrote. They were not far from the teaching of Delsarte when together they formulated a single aim: to liberate the human body from the fetters of meaningless conventions and give it the opportunity of becoming alive and expressive of the soul.

Work with Dalcroze challenged Appia's concepts of design and in 1909 he published his *Rhythmic Spaces* with the idea of an open performance space with levels and ramps – a corporeal space or living space for the moving actor. Laban must have known about this when he designed his own theatre and performance spaces. Appia's influence on Dalcroze encouraged him to pay more attention to working with groups instead of simply concentrating on individuals. The ultimate goal was the harmony of body and spirit and they felt it could best be achieved by a combination of ear training (listening), eurhythmics, improvisation and musical plasticity. Again there are elements of Delsarte, especially in some of the movements and postures.

In spite of some opposition, Dalcroze's reputation spread and in 1910 a firm of furniture manufacturers and estate agents offered to build him a specialist institute if he would bring his work to their newly created garden suburb at Hellerau, Dresden. Appia and Dalcroze prepared plans for an ambitious school and festival. The main auditorium realized a long ambition of Appia's – to unite in one space the audience seating and the performance area without any proscenium arch or front curtain.

In 1911 the Dalcroze Institute for Applied Rhythm was opened and the first festival was held in the summer of the following year when the dance drama *Echo and Narcissus* was performed together with the scene in Hades from Gluck's *Orpheus and Euridice*. Lighting was a prime feature of the effect – attention was focused on soloists and both dancing and singing choruses. Bernard Shaw, from under his music critic's hat, praised the production as 'one of the best'.

That festival and the work it entailed seems to have taken its toll on Dalcroze's principal piano teacher, and 'star' assistant, Suzanne Perrottet. (From the age of thirteen, she had trained under Dalcroze from his days at the Academy.) To recuperate, she had taken herself off for a fortnight to the sanatorium 'Die Weisse Hirsch' on the outskirts of Dresden. Also recuperating at the same time, in the same hotel, was Rudolf Laban. They met, exchanged ideas and found they had a great deal in common. They talked about movement and dance and even at that first encounter Laban must have learned a great deal about Dalcroze. Laban, however, had his own ideas and quickly persuaded the captivated Suzanne, arguing that dance was an art in its own right

which did not need music to release it. She was impressed
by his even more liberated approach. He told her not to copy
but to try always to be herself and remain true to her inner
creativity. When she returned to Dalcroze, she became
another of those who argued that the Eurhythmic approach
made movement, and so the dance, subservient to the music
when it should be unregulated and free.

So strong was Laban's pull on Perrottet that she tried
almost immediately to give notice and quit the Institute to
be with her new mentor. She was however under contract
and bound to work for a further twelve months. New
Dalcroze schools were opening in Budapest, Moscow and
Vienna and, given the choice, she decided to work out her
year's contract in Vienna. It was the plan for her then to
return to Laban and run a school with him for 'The New
Dance' which was to be dance independent music. Perrottet
was to use her musical knowledge, to improvise and
accompany.

Not long after Suzanne Perrottet met Laban in Dresden,
another of Dalcroze's students was also feeling dissatisfied
with her means of expression. Mary Wigman had been
attending the Hellerau Institute for two years, but found the
training tame and, with its close visualization of the score,
restrictive, unable to make room for her sense of dynamism
and freedom.

She knew Perrottet quite well, as she had been her teacher
of piano improvisation, and was 'stunned' to learn that she
was intending to leave Dalcroze since 'they were so close'. 'I
am leaving,' she told Wigman, 'because I have met this
wonderful man, Rudolf von Laban.'[10] That summer of 1913,
Wigman joined Laban and Perrottet in Ascona. Within a
few weeks of her arrival, she was offered a contract from
Dalcroze to join his teaching staff in Berlin but chose to stay
with Laban instead.

There can be no doubt, then, of Laban's awareness of the
theory and practice of Dalcroze, and Dalcroze for his part

must have felt the presence of Laban, who had taken two of his best people though he still held on to Marie Rambert, who became his assistant, and worked with Nijinsky and the Ballets Russes in their version of *The Rite of Spring*.

The First World War came a year later and brought the temporary closure of the Dalcroze Institute. Laban moved to Zurich. Then in 1915 Dalcroze reopened, adding a Department of Dance Education from which developed the Hellerau Dance Group which staged the first production of Bartok's *The Wooden Prince*.

A year or so later, Hanya Holm began studying with Dalcroze and on graduation became a teacher for him for a while. Then she too left, in her case having come under the spell of Mary Wigman's dancing. She joined her in Dresden as both dancer and teacher. And so the two traditions became interestingly intertwined. Dalcroze himself continued his teaching and research till his death in Geneva in 1950, though his Institute had transferred to Vienna in 1925. By this time, Laban was well established with his own theory and notation.

Carl Gustav Jung

Although Laban includes Jung's 1912 *Psychology of the Unconscious* amongst the bibliography listed at the end of *The Dancer's World* and although Laban and Jung worked in Switzerland at various times in both Zurich and Ascona, it is evident that Laban did not really become interested in the work of that psychotherapist until the 1950s.

The two men could have got on well together since several of their attitudes, circumstances and outlooks were similar. Carl Jung was born in 1875 (just six years after Laban) and died in 1961 (three years after Laban). His early years were spent in or near Basel, an historic town, which like Laban's home town, Pressburg, was surrounded by countryside.

Jung says there were times when he felt himself to be almost one with nature.

Jung was the son of a philologist and pastor, and the home he grew up in was rather unhappy as his mother and father were temperamentally unsuited. This meant that his, like Laban's, was a rather isolated childhood which led him to find refuge in a rich imaginative life, vivid dreams and ritualistic games.

Jung's father had a powerful influence on him, though in a very different way from Laban's. Even as a child, Carl Gustav set himself the task of restoring his father's lost faith and this became a mission throughout his life, influencing the development of his psychology. (Laban's life mission to improve the status of dance was also stimulated by his father's attitude.) Jung was a questioning child and though he did enjoy his early education, he found his secondary schooling unhappy and boring.

In his later teens he liked reading the philosophers, especially Pythagoras, Heraclitus, Empedocles and Plato, as he searched for help in understanding the world and what he considered was God's imperfect creation. Several of his early childhood experiences had religious connotations and links with nature which remained as influences underpinning his later quests and investigations.

At first, choice of a career seemed a problem. Though his father was against his reading theology, several of his uncles who were clergymen thought this the obvious choice. Towards the end of his schooldays, however, scientific interests began to develop and he eventually decided to go in for medicine. In 1895 he began his studies at Basel University, which he successfully completed in 1900. He then worked as an assistant at the Burghölzi Psychiatric Hospital while taking his doctorate with the University of Zurich. In his thesis he attempted to give a scientific explanation of occult phenomena.

Through his work at the mental hospital, he developed

association tests and also became interested in the strange fantasies his patients produced. In 1907 Jung published a book which attracted the interest of Freud and led to Jung being invited to join him in Vienna. A strong emotional friendship developed between the two and they worked closely together for some seven years in spite of reservations which Jung maintained with regard to certain of Freud's views.

In 1912 Jung published his *Psychology of the Unconscious*, which emphasized the differences between the two men with regard to the importance of incest and sexuality, and it was this that finally led to the break between them. In his own way, Jung took further ideas initiated by Freud: the importance of the history of the parents was developed into the importance of the history of the whole race and society in relation to the unconscious and its lead into spiritual progression. Additionally Jung made further studies of fantasies, visions and dreams and began to paint images from emotions and the unconscious, regarding them as having special significance.

Out of this work came his concept of the male and femaleness in everyone, identifying this as the *animus* and *anima*. His writing at this point seems to have had elements which Laban might have recognized: some described his *Psychology of the Unconscious* as mystical and worthless. Much of what he wrote seemed to lack scientific verification, being more akin to poetry.

In 1921, just prior to Laban moving to his years of intense dance practice in Hamburg, Jung published his *Psychological Types*. Laban, however, was not to become interested in this work for another 30 years, by which time he was already established in England and was developing his theory in relation to several other fields of investigation and expression.

It was in 1943 that an association began that was to draw him to some aspects of the psychology of Jung. Though

Laban and Lisa Ullmann had moved their base to Manchester, they still visited Dartington on teaching and lecturing commitments. Nearby, in Exeter, Dr H. Irene Champernowne and her husband had set up their centre for psychotherapy. Then, through a mutual acquaintance, John Trevelyan, Laban and Irene Champernowne met at one of the Dartington Hall courses. There were many other people there on that occasion and they did not find an opportunity to discuss Carl Jung until several years later (in 1950).

Both had been invited by the School of Occupational Therapy to speak at the YMCA in Great Russell Street; Irene Champernowne was speaking on the use of painting in remedial work and Laban talked about movement. It was then that they recognized each other as kindred spirits. At first, Irene Champernowne took her patients and students from her Withymead Centre to take part in Laban movement sessions at Dartington; then she invited him over to Withymead to run remedial movement sessions there.

On one of these occasions she drove him back to Dartington after the course and then the real exchange began. 'Rudolf didn't know much about the psychology of it all,' she said in an interview, 'but he showed a special interest in Jung's *Psychological Types*.'[11]

As usual, Laban was fortunate. He had found someone whose knowledge he could utilize. Irene Champernowne had a broad psychological background, having started out in the Freudian camp and then gone to Vienna to study under Adler. Following that, during some work in southern Germany, she read one of Jung's books and immediately wrote to him asking if she could become a student of his. At that point, in 1936, he was in Ascona, and he invited her to join him there. She studied in Switzerland with him and later took her PhD from the psychology department at London University, wanting to focus her thesis on Zurich and Jungian psychology.

One especially long drive in 1950 from Exeter to London

enabled Irene to talk to Laban at length about *Psychological Types* and out of this grew a great exchange – he gave her private lessons in movement, she told him about Jung's ideas on the unconscious, the shadow, the types, the approach to questions as teleological rather than causal investigation.

Jung builds on a long history of attempts to classify human beings according to type, going back to the Greeks. He first distinguishes two contrasting attitudes to the circumstances of life: extroverts, whose instinctive reaction is to say 'yes', and introverts, who more readily say 'no'. Extroverts demonstrate an outward flowing of the libido, a confidence in and affirmation of life, and an interest in people; while introverts are characterized more by an initial withdrawal, tending to prefer their own company and reflection rather than action. Jung uses these categories to refer to a person's predominant conscious attitude. A balanced adult would show equal aspects of both.

But we are individual and more complex than that. There are further psychological types which need to be distinguished. Jung maintains we make our relationships with the world through four main functions: the intellect, feelings, the senses and intuitions. Most of us have one function which is highly developed and another which is less so. When a reaction is pronounced, he speaks of a type.

For instance, some people think more than others. They regard the intellect as crucial in making decisions, and sorting things out. It is whether they are introverted or extroverted that will influence the nature and material of their thinking. The extrovert is interested in facts and the world of objective reality, whereas the introvert is more subjective. His/her thinking is less concerned with facts, more with ideas; it formulates theories, finds insights and creates imaginative narratives.

Laban's interest was first aroused when Irene began to explain to him why they, as two such apparent opposites, should be such kindred spirits. For example Laban noticed their different approaches to the simple task of arranging the room. 'When I put people anywhere,' Laban said, 'I do it according to angles and mathematical relationships to each other ... I see ... the whole group according to a mathematical pattern. You do it through your feeling, how it feels right.'[12] It did not take Laban long before his mind was carrying out its introspective thinking and making relationships with his own effort theory.

It is helpful to look at Laban himself through these psychological types. Clearly, he is predominantly extrovert but not, as we might rush to conclude, an extrovert thinker. He primarily functions through *intuition*. He is 'no respecter of custom and is often ruthless about other people's feeling or convictions when he is hot on the scent of something new ... often looks like a ruthless adventurer ... but he has his own morality based on loyalty to his intuitive view ... he sows but never reaps ... it is almost impossible for him to carry a thing through to the end ... personal relationships are weak; he finds it difficult to stick to one woman and home soon becomes a prison.'

His secondary function is that of the thinker, but here he is much more introverted. 'External facts are not the aim and origin of his thinking, although the introvert would often like to make it so appear ... it opens up prospects and yields insight ... its actual creative power is proved by the fact that this thinking can also create that idea which, though not present in the external facts, is yet the most suitable abstract expression of them ... He is not interested in outer reality ... does not notice what is going on or understand how other people think or feel.'

Dr Champernowne, asked to comment on Laban's personality from her standpoint as a Jungian, made some shrewd observations, noticing first that, although he was a warm and lovable man, good to make human personal contact with, he did not find it easy, was even perhaps afraid of close contact with people.

'We Jungians,' she went on, 'look at the archetypes that people live, and he goes very close to the archetype of the trickster . . . being an opportunist in a way and a bit of a wizard . . . intuitives are always in danger of the ego using intuition . . . manipulating life.' She added, 'It was a bit of genius, too, that made him take over war time circumstances and deal with movement in war situations such as factories and parachute jumping.'[13]

Withymead was an important link for Laban, for there, amongst the acquaintances of Irene Champernowne, he met William Carpenter and soon the two together were trying to translate aspects of Jungian theory into a new framework within the patterns of Laban's understanding of movement. Laban's intuition and introspective thinking were again at work.

7 Colleagues and the Exchange of Ideas

I have argued so far that Laban drew 'the basics of his insight' from practical experience and that this insight was tested and modified in the light of a number of forerunners on whose ideas he could build. But still, for him, the most important source of his knowledge is the dance itself, the sharing and exchange of ideas with other dancers and fellow workers.

In the period from 1910 to the outbreak of the Second World War, Laban influenced hundreds of individuals, many he worked with, some he danced with, some who danced for him and others who knew him and his work through being students of students, by reading his articles or articles about him. From the Second World War to the end of his life, Laban's influence spread not so much through the dance as through applied movement studies, the Laban Art of Movement Guild and the work of the Laban Centres in Manchester and Addlestone.

It is quite remarkable how many of the women he worked with (and they were mostly women) lived beyond eighty and some reached ninety years of age, continuing to be both physically and mentally active. Not only were many of those drawn to Laban attractive and physically fit for dance, but in addition the best of them grasped some of his theories and were able to dance them out in performance.

He certainly encountered 'hundreds of living enthusiasic dancers', though comparatively few were in any position to make much contribution to his ongoing search, or add to or challenge his theory when major developments were taking place. Yet there is a handful of outstanding individuals without whom he would not have travelled as far, or as famously, as he did. Included here are five of those key colleagues.

Mary Wigman

Of the people with whom he worked before 1920, Laban mentions some by name for 'warmest thanks' in the final section of his book *The Dancer's World* as 'assistants in my search and endeavour', and goes on 'I name here, above all, the dancer, Mary Wigman.'[14] Laban gives her pride of place, more as an exponent of the new dance (and therefore of his theories) than as someone who is challenging them.

Wigman exemplifies the new Laban dancer – not simply light and dexterous in dancing but able to communicate strong physical emotion. Laban first quotes Maria Benemann, from a Weimar article: 'Mary Wigman, as a sexually strong woman, made the first great move. She acknowledges the body in all its truth with the full sharpness and clarity of a strong mind. Mary Wigman's dance is a storm dictating, that is how I want it and that is how it will be. It is life-demanding at the same time as it surges forth power from the universe of her ego.'[15]

Then he goes on to quote from a Dresden newspaper echoing the same recognition of a dancer who employs her whole being, body, feelings and spirit, taking the audience to where 'physical existence reaches the cosmic world'. The critic recognizes that these are no accidental achievements and seems to emphasize those especially Labanian elements: 'Here we have innermost harmony . . . not just a few poses with a few variations. Here there are no dead spots, breaks or truncations. The secret of this dance lies in the creation of dance gesture; in the uninhibited flow of the turn, the stride, the outward swing of the hand. There is a life in these arms and hands that is incomparable in its richness and power. The intensity of this physical expression goes beyond our experience so far . . . With Mary Wigman we herald a new epoch in the art of the dance.' It was one thing for Laban to have a theory and to write about it, but here was an individual who could personify the change of attitude and response.

Born Marie Wiegmann in Hannover on 13 November 1886, she was seven years Laban's junior and like him was a traveller with 'a deep love of earth and sky and sea'. Like him also, she was a searcher, not knowing quite where she would arrive nor what she might find. On her own she found that movement helped to express her feelings but she too found parental opposition to her suggestion of a dancing career; in fact, her mother did not wish her to have a career at all. 'When I finished school,' she reminisces in her *Mary Wigman Book*, 'I was still seeking . . . I adventured into the arts studying music, singing. Then I heard of the Dalcroze school in Hellerau where an attempt was being made to co-ordinate musical rhythm with bodily rhythm.' She enrolled.

For two years she studied the piano there and easily passed the first stage. Then she took the advanced exam within the next six weeks and, though tired and exhausted, managed to scrape through and remain highly thought of by Dalcroze himself.

But Mary Wigman did not think so highly of the Dalcroze Institute. She felt Eurhythmics was too wooden, and there was not enough pure dance for her. As she records, she did what she was told and spent all the non-school hours dancing back at her lodgings.

She was a friend of the painter Emil Nolde and it was he who recommended that she go to Laban. 'He moves as you do,' he said, 'and dances as you do, without music.'[16] The only thing that she lacked to undertake further training was money. She had tenacity, imagination, enterprise and, above all, a desire to further her practice and understanding of the dance.

Her period of training with Jaques-Dalcroze had, on one level, been so successful that, even as she sought out Laban in Ascona, a contract arrived for her signature at the local post office, offering her charge of the School of Eurhythmics in Berlin.

It was 1913 and she was twenty-seven years old. In those days, professional dance training meant classical ballet and students had usually begun their dance schooling by the age of ten. But classical ballet 'was not my language', she declares. 'Mannered and stilted, it could never tell what I had to say.' She felt that she had grown beyond the limitations of the Dalcroze method so there could be no answer there – she turned to Rudolf von Laban as 'the only and great experimenter in the dance'.[17]

They came together at what seems to have been the right time for both of them. He was thirty-four; she twenty-seven; each on the threshold of a new professional world – dance, not as it had been practised but as it might become. He, with a vision, with vitality, with charm, with a driving passion to open up physical expression and show how it could communicate; she, with a dream, with a drive, an ambition, an intensity needing to find the means of greater physical expression and, with her whole body, speak it aloud powerfully to the whole world. She saw in him a teacher, a guide, the moving spirit to show her the way into self-discovery and growth. He saw in her an adventurer, a dancer (against the dainty mould of the tall, upright classical dancer), a strong, vigorous and rhythmic performer, who could give his vision a reality, who with him could discover just what the new instrument was capable of and how it could create an experience well beyond anything so far imagined.

That first summer together they improvised, explored and experimented. The small but varied group of that Ascona summer course enjoyed the glorious open-air landscape as, sometimes naked, they ran and leapt and created group and solo dances. They danced to music and without it; they danced to drum-beats, to words, to poems. They drew, they gardened, they carried out their domestic chores, prepared and ate their vegetarian meals. Day by day, everyone was making discoveries. Wigman did not accept it all without reaction but could not help being overcome by the 'inescapable charm' of her teacher, Laban.

She knew, however, that it was a wonderful introduction to Laban's philosophy of life as well as to his approaches to dance training and the liberation of the artist within. She appreciated it more because it was not a system by superimposition but a system for freeing the individual so that each could discover his or her own potential and develop his or her own technique and individual style of dancing.

In the autumn of that first year Wigman was teaching for Laban in Munich while he was ill as well as preparing dances for her first public performances. She was an immediate success and she knew that her career as a dancer had begun. Laban's following was also growing.

The following summer, it was a much bigger group that met in Ascona and more exciting work continued with talk of a full-time dance theatre until the sky darkened with the clouds of unrest and the First World War broke out. People quickly left but Wigman remained and it was then that she probably came to know Laban best.

Laban was working on an exercise system based on the function of the joints and on the tension and relaxation of the human body's musculature. By the outbreak of the First World War, his swings and scales had been clearly defined, forming the basis of his 'Theory of Harmony of Movement', but he was still determinedly struggling with the detail of his system of dance notation.

Though not always fully understanding what was going

on in Laban's mind, Mary Wigman worked ceaselessly with him, caring less about his theory, more about her creation and communication. In a sense, she was his guinea pig. 'I became the first victim to help prove his theoretical finding,' she says in *The Mary Wigman Book*

They met daily. Laban spread his drawings and notes over the table and floor, leaving her only a tiny space for practical demonstrations. 'This was his great dream to be realized: an analysis of movement and the experiment of translating it into signs as a cross-, bar-, or point-system, in a series of lines or curves. He repeatedly designed and rejected, always starting again from the beginning.'[18]

She thought the world of him and, as she says, would have done anything he asked. He thought the world of her and asked her to do almost anything. He relied upon her teaching when he became bored and left her to finish off many a class; he relied upon her acting when no one else could cope with Brandenburg's dance-drama text; he criticized, carped at and complimented her dancing but, all along, he seemed fully aware that there was greatness around.

With the end of the war the time came when, Mary Wigman felt quite naturally, they should part company and follow their separate paths. 'With his manifold tasks and interests, Laban needed a much broader field than I could ever have covered.'[19] She took from him all the theory that he had so far evolved and continued to work on it with intensity, fashioning it into her own system. Wigman seemingly went off on her own way but she was only doing what Laban had always preached – 'take from my work what you can and make it yours.'[20] Shrewdly, she combined something of Dalcroze with all that she had so far learnt and caught from Laban. She developed what came to be called 'Dance Gymnastics', an entirely natural system of rhythmic exercises. Before her was a great career of solo dancing throughout Europe and the States, running her own school, choreographing, teaching and nurturing other great talents.

Even though the subsequent years brought some moments of rivalry and even jealousy between the two, they ultimately came back together again with mutual respect and affection. She died in hospital in Berlin in September 1983, still able to recall so much of those early days with Laban. Her mind remained clear and active to the end. Within a few days of her death, when this great dancer was lying in hospital, her mind still danced though her body was crippled with pain. She knew all that was going on and as she looked up to the writer who had come to visit her she said, 'You have come all this way to see half a corpse.'[21] She smiled and her eyes still shone with understanding.

She always saw Laban as the person who had given her enough technical training for her to be able to make her own way; he knew that no one would ever again dance out his ideas with such belief and conviction or quite so powerfully extend the name and reputation of Laban amongst professional dancers.

Dussia Bereska

Of all the women who worked with Laban between the wars, one is especially important in the position she held during a most crucial period of the evolution of his thought and its expression in both theory and practice – that is Dussia Bereska. Even though her actual contribution is difficult to assess, few would deny that she exercised considerable influence. Her position was exceptional and she and Laban supported each other through thick and thin.

Of Russian origin, Olga Feldt-Bereska, like some others, came to Laban as a pupil and remained to live with him, bear his daughter and work with him for over a decade. She first joined the Laban circle as a student, in Ascona, Switzerland, in 1916, remaining to work with him in Zurich as a very special colleague and companion. Even Jooss, who acknowledged that he was jealous of her position, recognized their relationship as 'beautiful, quite marvellous'.[22]

Those First World War years gave Laban a chance to clarify and develop much of his basic theory. Bereska joined him for training while the theory was evolving. Wigman left to pursue her own career in 1918–19 and it seems that Bereska then became the person closest to Laban and the one he, from then on, used a great deal to test out some of his ideas in practical movement terms. Laban's wife had left Switzerland late in 1919 to return with their young family to Munich, regarding it as a formal separation. Bereska was in Nuremberg and Laban joined her there. The movement was symbolic.

Like Wigman, she had quite a strong personality but did not push herself for her own or her career's sake. She was altogether a different kind of dancer – elegant, delicate, less vigorous but with most expressive gestures. She impressed people with her regal attitude and upright carriage and seemed generally to exude an air of being sure of her position in the Laban circle. She was a great buffer for Laban, keeping others out of his way whenever possible.

She was a complex and complicated character. To some (like Jooss), she seemed proud and aloof, always loyal to Laban. His contemporaries, Jooss said, thought of her as a kind of Artemis figure who would never divulge her feelings nor hint at anything she might be suffering. Her teaching was popular and effective and most pupils liked her. Laban's respect for her and the trust he placed in her are reflected in the fact that, in spite of the problems, they stayed working alongside each other for some thirteen years.

The final decade of those years, the period from 1919 to 1929, was one of fundamental and feverish pursuit. Those times were the great ones for clarifying theory and putting it into practice through a flurry of activity: training young dancers and building performance work both for its own sake and setting up experiments in genre; establishing Laban Schools throughout Europe; extending the theoretical understanding in courses and lectures; finalizing his system of Kinetographie; consolidating a better status for dance and dancers and Publishing ideas in books and articles in German.

Bereska seems to have had some direct involvement in all of these areas, but she made a very special contribution to training dancers and developing a company. Whenever Laban was away (and he travelled a great deal for one reason or another), he left Bereska in charge.

Performance

Laban acknowledges Bereska in *The Dancer's World* simply as 'a dancer and pantomime actress'. According to Jooss, she was competent but not a good dancer, though she sometimes appeared as principal or solo dancer, given movements that she could perform well. Other people, better dancers like Gertrud Loeszer and Hertha Feist, danced directly with Laban, but Bereska was there both dancing with him and helping him in the running of the company. She was eventually given full responsibility for the Kammertanzbühne.

From Zurich, she went with Laban to Stuttgart and helped him found the Dance Theatre. In his unpublished 'Rudolf von Laban and the Rise of Modern Dance Drama', Fritz Boehme points out how this new concept nurtured many young people who were later to prove themselves in the world of dance and that it was under the joint leadership of Laban and Bereska.

By this point, she was already established as a company teacher, taking classes and working with small groups. She was with Laban in Mannheim, Gleschendorf and then Hamburg, where she looked after the training with the company. At first, the company set up in a house in

Runsbeck, a suburb of Hamburg, but performed in principal theatres in the city itself. Then, through the patronage of the owner of Nivea skin cream, they were able to hire the upper part of the restaurant in the Zoological Gardens which remained their home until the summer of 1929. There they had three large studios, one of which they converted into a theatre with a stage at one end.

This was dance pioneering of a revolutionary sort. Laban, with Bereska, established a two-week repertory during which the company built up a programme and performed it three times each week for two weeks. While performing one programme they were working on the next. It must have been a punishing but greatly rewarding experience for the dancers, and Kurt Jooss, who was part of the first company, pays tribute to it as excellent professional training.

Bereska went on most of the tours during that period, sometimes with the full company, sometimes taking the chamber dance group. She was an artist and could be a temperamental performer but what made things most problematic for those around her was that, when things were going badly, she tended to find comfort in cognac, which she drank like water. Over the years, she became more addicted to alcohol and could be hours, days, even weeks out of action.

Sometimes she would even go on stage drunk. There were occasions when the company had quite a hard time with her, having to pass her from one to the other to keep her upright. On one occasion, in Hamburg, during the time that Laban was off doing one of his tours and recitals with Loeszer and Jooss was acting as company manager, Bereska was dancing a tragic role and sailed across the stage with merry abandon and a totally inappropriate facial expression. They tried everything from flashing the lights to shaking her but she remained smilingly oblivious to all their signals. Finally, when the audience burst into laughter, they simply had to lower the curtain.

Such incidents, however, did not put her permanently out of action nor out of favour, and she continued to make valuable contributions almost to the end of the decade.

Extending Dance Boundaries

Bereska worked jointly with Laban in evolving the choreography for a number of ballets. Her collaborative role is credited in the programmes of several including *Orchidée*, *The Magic Garden*, *The Dragon-slayer*, *Terpsichore*, *Westliche Contemporains*, *The Fool's Mirror* and *Green Clowns*. She was acknowledged as Laban's Assistant for *Ritterballet*.

This was the period when Laban and others in Germany were attempting to bring several of the arts together into a single theatre experience. Laban, together with Vilma Monckeberg from the University of Hamburg, was experimenting with moving and speaking choruses or choirs in large-scale productions like *Prometheus*, *A Midsummer Night's Dream*, Gluck's *Don Juan* and *Faust's Erlösung*, based on Goethe's *Faust, Part II*. The idea of a dance oratorio was explored to put into practice the synthesis of dance, sound, word, which became a kind of slogan at this time.

Laban was stretching, stimulating a fresh look at the very concept of ballet. Dance for him was the combining root of art, basic, natural and liberated from the rigid form-language of much of the ballet he saw around him. He was eager to demonstrate that there were no themes or subjects which could not be taken on by the dance and showed a special concern for the artistic expression of some of those foundations laid down in his early experiences.

Through his dance theatre, he was anxious to explore myth rather than fairy-tale, man's link with nature and the universe in a philosophic rather than a sentimental approach, and of course, instead of formal steps, ornamental gestures and figures, the very essence and meaning of movement itself.

He was equally challenging when it came to style and genre. He was interested in the brief solo dance, the duo and so on and just as vigorously the full chorus epic. Expressive dance, he showed, could be tragic or comic, stylized or free-form. Dance could be formal, abstract ballet or theatrical dance-drama. It could be part of a range of festivities from concerts to cabarets, from divertissement to dervishes, from pantomimes to pageants. Dance could have its own special-ized theatre, simply serve the opera or lead the Olympic Games.

At almost every stage, there was Bereska at his side or keeping things going at another venue. As well as working and dancing with the company, Bereska was also helping to arrange their tours throughout Germany in 1923 and 1924. She was with them on their financially catastrophic tour of Yugoslavia. She was a good organizer and seemed to enjoy it.

Laban Schools

Laban's work was spreading through the establishment of Labanschulen all over Europe. In 1924, Bereska with others was instrumental in setting up the Laban School in Rome. On return to Hamburg we find her running the Kammer-tanzbühne which began performances in the autumn of 1925, first in the theatre in the Zoo and then on tour. In 1929 she left to run the Laban School in Paris.

Theory

Bereska seems to have been a woman who, unlike Wigman, held a genuine interest in Laban's theory both of dance and what it should/could be, and his more abstract movement ideas. Both Jooss and Snell recognize that she regularly exchanged ideas with Laban as the theory developed and, what is more, the suggestions she made often turned out to be very significant. She showed less interest in the Choreutics approach. Her particular involvement was with Eukinetics – the expression, the dynamics, the rhythms (later called effort and effort-shape). At one point, Laban said that all of Eukinetics was Bereska's invention and certainly much of the work was first tried out with her.

She also assisted Laban in the development of the notation and here too may have contributed key elements and approaches. Laban told Jooss that the telescopic sign was her idea. In the spring of 1927 she went to Berlin to help establish the Choreographic Institute.

Status

Bereska worked with Laban to establish a meeting-ground for dancers of all persuasions which culminated in the First Dancers' Congress held in Magdeburg in the summer of 1927. It was at this Congress that Laban gave his paper on 'Dance as a work of Art'.

Publications

The years 1920–30 mark the period when Laban was most prolific in his writing. He began the decade with the publication of his major book *The Dancer's World* and continued to write articles covering various aspects of dance, such as dance as theatre, as art, as religion. There are articles on movement choirs, choreography and festivals. In 1926, he brought out three books: *Gymnastics and Dance, Children's Gymnastics and Dance*, and *Choreography*. There are several articles on aspects of dance notation.

In *The Dancer's World*, Laban acknowledges that 'Bereska has, through her co-operation, contributed to this work'. It was most likely she who prepared the manuscript for the publishers and no doubt assisted through discussion in helping to find the final form of the book. He had been working on the book for almost two years, during most of which time Bereska had been with him. Usually Laban prepared publications assisted by others and the close relationship between him and Bereska gives rise to the belief that she worked with him 'through her co-operation'[23] during a good deal of this highly productive period.

Bereska's drinking gradually got the better of her and her relationship with Laban became more and more difficult. Finally, she and Laban decided to part company – though clearly in a mood which maintained respect, for she went off to Paris to found and run the Laban school in 1929 and was joined by Snell a short time later. This was where Laban went first when he finally escaped from the Nazis.

Kurt Jooss

Laban found it less easy to build close working-relationships with men, but it is unlikely that he would be remembered or have become so renowned had it not been for the part in his life played by Kurt Jooss.

Born in Germany, in Wasseralfingen, at the turn of the century (12 January, 1901), Kurt Jooss was the son of farming parents who at first hoped he would follow in their footsteps. Jooss at eighteen, having just finished his schooling and with a brief acquaintance with photography, chose, however, to remain for a while undecided about his career. Through the Youth Movement, he had found plenty of outlets for his delight in acting, dancing and music. His introduction to Laban's ideas was through an article about him and his work in *Body Building as an Art and Obligation* by Fritz Hanna Winther, which came out in 1919.

He enrolled first in the local but prestigious Academy of Music and then found his way to the Stuttgart Dramatic Academy in 1920. It was here, from the dancing teacher, that he again heard of and first met Laban. Laban, however, was not interested in teaching and was certainly not keen, at that point, to foster Jooss's enthusiasm. But Jooss was determined and, in spite of the obstacles, managed to pursuade Laban to teach him and a few others for five months.

Jooss had previously promised his father that he would study farm management and so, at the end of that time, left to attend an agricultural college near Ulm. His idea had been eventually to establish an arts school in the country on a site which was part of the family farm. When his father died shortly afterwards, Jooss returned home to Wasseralfin-gen and the farm he might inherit. He stayed some months with his mother and during that time paid a visit to Stuttgart to see Mary Wigman's recital there. He was so impressed, he said, that it was that experience which finally tipped the balance. Without delay, he sought out Laban, in Stuttgart.

This time (in the autumn of 1921), Jooss actually joined Laban and his other students in Mannheim where they were performing the 'Bacchanale' in the Paris version of *Tann-häuser*. Jooss was quickly given a part to dance that would not upset the rest of the choreography which was already well advanced in rehearsal. Early the following year, the company went to Hamburg, where Jooss became an estab-lished part of the group who performed regularly in the Theater am Zoo, in major theatres of Hamburg and on tour during 1922–3.

Laban gave a great deal to Jooss, but just as importantly Laban owed a great deal to Jooss. From their first meeting, Jooss, too, came directly under Laban's spell. 'He had a radiance', he commented when, more than 50 years later, he talked about their first meeting. 'Such an extraordinary personality that everyone became intoxicated by him.'[24]

Over and over again Jooss comments 'he was a god,' and that early infatuation never died. Those Hamburg years with Laban laid the foundations for Jooss's dancing and directing career, but happily (for both of them) there were two other factors involved: Jooss had undoubted natural gifts and talents (which Laban's training brought out and developed) and that was coupled with what seemed like a charmed life. Jooss felt his life was, 'like a fairy-tale', so much good fortune attended his career. Laban had little luck of his own but, characteristically, Jooss saw to it that Laban shared his.

From the very beginning, Laban evolved a training approach which dancers like Jooss used as their future approach – classwork, theoretical discussion, experimental workshops, rehearsals and performances. Learning continued through rehearsals and performances every bit as much as through classes and workshops. During that early period, Fritz Boehme calculates that there were no fewer than 185 performances which, besides Hamburg, took the company to Munich, Berlin and Silesia.

Laban was a master of improvisation and not only did he choreograph by means of it, but it was also at the heart of his teaching. Jooss responded to it and though he was not in Bereska's favoured position, he soon became one of Laban's leading male dancers. It was he who gradually persuaded Laban himself to take to the stage rather than excusing himself because he was 'not on form' or 'not in training'. Although Jooss was aware that Laban would not produce great jumps or leaps, he was impressed by 'his terrific stage presence,' together with the quiet, simple movements he gave himself and the outstanding expressiveness of Laban's arms and hands. 'He had marvellous hands,' Jooss later declared. 'It was as if fire came from them when they were in motion.'[25] Jooss was especially proud when he danced opposite him.

Laban began to entrust Jooss with choreography and Jooss also taught a number of classes. He soon came to be regarded as Laban's assistant and carried out research projects as well as being given theoretical problems to solve. He did not find Laban easy to work with, but Jooss tolerated harsh criticism and much more because of his respect for Laban's artistic and innovative genius. All, however, did not go as Jooss would have liked. It was a professional association but never as close as the young Jooss would have liked.

Jooss could be rebellious and was jealous of the position held by people like Bereska and Gertrud Loeszer. Yet relationships between them did not become difficult until the spring of 1924, when Laban became ill again and went off for six weeks to the Riviera to recuperate. He left Jooss with work to prepare for the new season's repertoire.

On his return, Laban was unhappy with the results and made it clear to Jooss that he was out of favour: he gave Jooss some very scathing criticism about a solo piece on which he had been working and asked Loeszer to finish off choreography which Jooss had all but completed. Laban also chose not to select him for the forthcoming tour of Yugoslavia. Jooss was devastated, feeling that it would be hard to continue to work with the company in such an atmosphere.

Later he was, like Mary Wigman, happy to rationalize his departure as 'the natural desire for weaning'.[26] In any case, he began to look for other positions and was soon offered the post of ballet-master at the Munster Theatre, which had already established a reputation as the most avant-garde theatre in Germany. When Laban heard of the offer, he tried to stop Jooss from taking it up, maintaining that he owed much to his master. But Jooss felt that he had already been 'thrown out' by Laban and so, reluctantly making a break, took up the job in Munster. Here, with his close friend Sigurd Leeder, Aino Siimola (whom he married in 1929), the designer Hein Heckroth and the musician Frederic Cohen, Jooss set up his Neue Tanzbühne as a separate department at Munster, experimenting and producing dance theatre – all very much in the Laban tradition.

For a while the paths of Laban and Jooss only crossed

from time to time. Jooss continued to dance and choreograph but there came a point when he and Leeder felt that they wanted to test out Laban theory against the more ingrained classical approach, a quest which took them to Paris and Vienna. Paradoxically this seemed, if anything, to strengthen their belief in Laban's ideas, and Jooss remained ever on the look-out for chances of reconciliation with his master.

In 1927, Jooss became director of dance at the newly formed Essen Folkwang School and Sigurd Leeder its principal teacher. This was the year of the First Dancers' Congress at which, in spite of some remaining estrangement, Jooss and Laban met. Jooss took on the organization of the Congress for the following year and actually hosted it at Essen. It was on this occasion that Laban formally offered his system of notation. While it was still in its early stages of development, Jooss and Leeder had experimented and contributed valuable ideas. In 1928 Jooss invited Laban to link his Central School with Folkwang.

By this time, Marie Luise Lieschke, wife of an eye surgeon from Plauen, had shown considerable interest in Laban and his work and devoted much of her energy and patronage to helping Laban on to a firmer financial footing. Jooss got on well with her and she used her sway with Laban to help talk him into establishing the headquarters for his work at Essen where Jooss was Director.

1929 saw the move of the Central Laban School to Essen to combine with the Folkwang School and Laban, as its chief examiner, received an annual stipend. In December it was Laban's fiftieth birthday, and at the celebrations held at Essen the Jooss company danced *Pavane*, which Jooss had created as his present for Laban.

In the following year, Jooss became the ballet-master of the Essen Opera House with his company, the Folkwang Tanzbühne (the nucleus of which was the Laban-influenced group from Munster). In April, Jooss revived Laban's

Gaukelei and presented it at the Third Dancers' Congress, held in Munich, much to Laban's delight. That same year Laban began his association as choreographer with the Bühnenfestspiele at Bayreuth and was pleased to use the Folkwangtanzbühne in his dances for Wagner's *Tannhäuser*, with Jooss working alongside him. Jooss also added his voice to those arguing that Laban should be the new ballet-master to the Berlin State Opera in Unter den Linden and they eventually won the day. It was taking time, but the rift between Jooss and Laban was beginning to heal.

The complete reinstatement of Jooss to Laban's favour came in 1932. At the first ever international choreographic competition, held in Paris, Jooss and his Folkwangtanz-bühne were awarded the first prize for *The Green Table*. It was a great moment for Jooss, it was a great moment for the company, it was a great moment for modern ballet, and for Laban it was a triumph of so many of his ideas. The Laban approach to ballet and choreography now had international acknowledgement.

The wealthy Swedish art patron Rolf de Maré, after the collapse of his own company, had established Les Archives Internationales de la Danse in 1931. The following year, this organization held their first competition for choreographers, for the best original ballet.

Twenty-one companies (mainly classical) took part, from ten different nations, the competition spreading over three evenings. Jooss's initial reaction to those who urged him to enter was that he had nothing appropriate and so must decline. Eventually, however, a number of ideas at the back of his mind came together and intensive rehearsals took place over a period of six weeks preceeding the competition. From this intense period *The Green Table* was born. The main line of action and themes were all Jooss; the concept and choreography were Jooss's evocation of the theory and practice of Rudolf Laban:

1. The dancing, which put into practice Laban's theories of movement (choreutics and eukinetics), was powerfully expressive rather than decorative dance movement, each moment of which was telling.
2. No *corps de ballet* but a real company, which had been trained to discover the rhythm within and how to communicate it in the service of the dance and each other.
3. The piece was dramatic; a simple plot with focus on character and the interplay of character.
4. A thoroughly unromantic, tragic theme: human greed and its outcome in death and deprivation – with all the Noverre seriousness of purpose. On the one hand harking back to the First World War, while on the other horrifyingly prophetic, being first performed the year before Hitler became Chancellor and concentration camps were initiated.
5. The simplest of décor – so placing emphasis on the dancers – no painted cloths, but effective employment of flags and the three-dimensional table round which the power-seeking politicians gathered at the beginning and the end.
6. Modern costumes which were basic but with good colour contrasts.
7. The use (at the beginning and end) of masks for sharp and clear communication (as well as for economy of personnel).
8. A rejection of the offered sixteen-piece orchestra in preference for the directness and simplicity of two pianos and a Kurt Weill-influenced score.

The Green Table was a huge success and established that modern dance could be about significant, contemporary matters; less about display, more about genuine inner feeling and commitment. L. Franc Scheuer reported in the *Dancing Times* that it 'was easily the outstanding revelation of the series and long will one recall the thunderous applause that greeted it'.

For Jooss and Laban, it was the warmest reuniting and immediately Jooss shared his success with Laban. In a sense, both had obtained recognition in the field of choreography and from that point on the reputation of Laban as a modern dance innovator began to spread world-wide.

Neither Laban nor Jooss could have had any idea in their moment of joy of the dark shadow moving inexorably towards them both. Winning the competition and being fully reconciled came none too soon. Within a year, Jooss was forced out of Germany by the Nazis. Fortunately, however, the prestigious choreographic prize led to an invitation to set up a dance school and company base at Dartington Hall.

Jooss continued to think about Laban and tried to persuade him to leave Germany; yet, as we have seen, in spite of the restrictions under Goebbels, Laban clung on, trying to establish dance as a respectable and respected art. When the break with Germany finally came, Laban made for Paris and Bereska. Bereska was in no state to look after him. Laban was not only ill but disillusioned; his life's work seemed in total ruins and he had neither strength nor will to start again.

Once more Jooss shared his good fortune with his old mentor. In the winter of 1937, he visited Laban in Paris and invited him to make his future home in Dartington. The following January, Laban (now fifty-eight) arrived and stayed as Jooss's guest. It was just in time, for the Second World War broke out little more than a year later. For two and a half years Laban had the hospitality of Jooss's home and a summerhouse where he could set up his 'magician's room'. Jooss helped nurse him back to health, gave him facilities to study geometric and crystal forms and reinvigorated his appetite for life. Jooss himself had only limited time to spend with Laban but, without knowing it, he had nurtured someone who was to be instrumental in ensuring that Laban's work safely entered its next phase. Had it not been for his move to Jooss and England, Laban's work might have been more obscured and limited than it is today.

Albrecht Knust

The dancer Albrecht Knust was a diligent, methodical, devoted worker. He was self-effacing, kind, concerned and understanding, without the personal ambition of people like Jooss as choreographer, or Wigman as dancer, or even Ullmann as teacher. He was not, as so many others were, emotionally in thrall to Laban; he was more absorbed by Laban theory. He devoted much of his energies and life to serving the ideas, especially the evolution of the Laban-inspired script (Kinetographie Laban) that would record dance works and movement of all kinds.

Knust worked hard in developing amateur and folk-dance groups, but, essentially a backroom boy, he remained more often behind the follow spot than actually in it. On the professional side, he was the support dancer, the substitute ballet-master, the stand-by trainer, the dedicated but unobtrusive teacher. When other people were ill, fell out of favour, lost interest, he was there to be called upon. And he always met the occasion without drawing attention to his action. His level head and capacity to rise above dispute, or circumvent it, made him the one who was often given the responsibility without receiving much of the fame.

Albrecht Knust was born in October 1896. He remained close to his family, especially his mother, his sister and her husband who in times of hardship (and he had a number of these) helped house or support him. Not quite eighteen years old by the time France, Belgium and Britain were at war with his native Germany, Knust was drafted into the army but must have been a terrible misfit, even though he acknowledged that he became stronger if stiffer because of the work he had been put to. During the First World War, Laban remained in neutral Switzerland.

After the war, in 1920, Laban had published *The Dancer's World* and this, with other news of his reputation, led Knust to him. Knust joined the recently formed Laban Dance Company, in 1921, just before Jooss returned to Laban after the death of his father. Immediately, he was drafted into preparing for the 'Bacchanale' for Wagner's *Tannhäuser* to be performed at the National Theatre of Mannheim where they all went a fortnight later. Knust probably knew he was not a gifted dancer, but he derived a great deal of understanding from the experience, even though his part in this important première was limited to crawling close to the floor.

Nevertheless, Knust had a rare feeling for and understanding of the dance, so it was not long before Laban appreciated his strengths. After the collapse, in 1924, of the Tanzbühne Laban tour in Yugoslavia, it was important for Laban to reorganize his remaining personnel. Knust was given responsibility for the Hamburg Bewegungschöre (movement choir). That was the year in which Laban published his major statement on the idea of the movement choir and Knust continued to pioneer in this field especially with lay movement groups.

Knust's other main interest was in dance notation. Laban had aready clarified the basic ideas of the script for his Kinetographie method and Knust became one of the key figures in preparing the principles of Kinetographie for publication in 1928. Knust went on to sort out many of the problems of notation which still remained. In June 1927, he had made the first score of a dance, *Titan*, to be written in Laban's script and founded the Hamburg Dance Notation Bureau in order to promulgate Laban's notation system. From this point on, he spent much of his energy in further development and clarification of dance and movement notation. In the autumn of 1928 Laban had set up a Central School in Berlin as part of the Choreographic Institute and he asked Knust to organize and direct the work there.

The summer of 1930 saw Laban running a summer course at Bayreuth and working as choreographer to the Wagner Festival. Knust was sent in his place to the UK to run courses in the name of Laban at Bedford College and to introduce Laban's ideas to the Imperial Society of Teachers of Dancing. This was the first official statement of Laban's principles in England, though Anny Fligg and Anny Boalth, both former students of Laban, had previously come to the UK to teach.

That same year, the Third Dancers' Congress was held, this time in Munich, for which Knust prepared a movement choir demonstration as well as contributing to the exhibition of Laban's notation at the Theatre Museum in Munich. Knust had used notation so that colleagues could rehearse sections of the work – the first time the script was used to prepare and recreate a work of Laban's. He also went on to evolve a method of notation for group dances which he later published. The interest created by this work greatly encouraged Knust and so he founded the Hamburg Dance Notation Bureau.

In spite of a great deal of enthusiasm, these were difficult times. Besides developing Laban's ideas on his own, Knust was trying to earn a living from teaching and directing. But income was scarce. Eager students, whether full- or part-time, found it a struggle to pay the fees. When Kurt Jooss fled Germany with his company in 1934, Knust was asked to take over the direction of the Department of Dance at the Folkwang School in Essen. However, the political situation proved difficult and, after a year, intrigues became so fierce that Knust had to leave what remained of the Folkwang in Essen. By this stage, Laban had left his post as choreographer to the Berlin State Opera to become the director of the Deutsche Tanzbühne under the Ministry of Propaganda. He was now in charge of dance and movement for the whole of Germany, so Knust pleaded to him for help, hoping to find work where he could concentrate on various aspects of notation. This was the opportunity for Laban to create the Berlin Dance Notation Bureau and Knust was appointed to run it.

In addition, Laban had been asked to choreograph the

incidental dances for Wagner's *Rienzi* at Waldoper, Zoppot, near Danzig, but could not leave his Berlin duties. Laban told Knust what he wanted – three choirs, each of thirty people, performing group dances. For a week Knust took down the notation as it came from Laban's choreographic ideas and for the first time created a score for a Laban ballet suite *before* it was rehearsed and performed. Knust then went off to work with the dancers and the piece was premièred in May of that year.

That summer Knust spent teaching and giving exhibitions of notation on a course set up by Laban under the Ministry of Propaganda for out-of-work dancers. The following year, Knust worked alongside Irmgard Bartenieff, translating the old Feuillet-notated dances into the notation of the Laban system.

Laban was already making festival preparations for the 1936 Olympic Games and had planned the dance programme for *Vom Tauwind und der neuen Freude* [*From the Warm Wind and the New Joy*], drawing up rough sketches of the flow plans and left the group leaders to invent the dances. He gave Knust the task of controlling and co-ordinating the dances, so he called the group leaders for a weekend to outline the procedure and then visited them from time to time in different parts of the country. At the end of the rehearsal period, Knust organized a week's rehearsals in Berlin, culminating in the dress rehearsal which Goebbels visited.

Cancelling the performance was only the first of Goebbels' actions. Laban instantly became *persona non grata*. Knust, with other dance teachers, was summoned to Berlin and they were instructed to change their ways of teaching. The penalty for infringing this ban was the concentration camp. Knust knew no other way of teaching, and had already made Kinetographie Laban his main focus.

For a time he tried to continue quietly, taking short courses and teaching small groups. But Nazi informers infiltrated his classes and on more than one occasion he was given warnings and issued with heavy threats until eventually he was left with no way of making a livelihood. After the night of the fires and the burning of Jewish synagogues, the situation became more and more oppressive.

In 1937 Knust did manage to get to Dartington for a few months to discuss the first draft of his *Handbook of Kinetography Laban* [sic] with Jooss and Sigurd Leeder. He did not, of course, tell the Nazis his real reason for undertaking the journey, but the visit enabled an exchange of ideas just before the great cut-off came.

Later, in 1938, back in Germany he received an invitation from Jooss to join him in Dartington on a permanent basis, but it came too late. The German authorities refused to grant him permission to leave. Without a job and with little means of earning a living, Knust went again to live with his sister and brother-in-law until fortune turned and he received an invitation from a former student who had just been appointed to the post of ballet-master at the Munich State Opera House.

In spite of the embargo on all Laban's work, Knust became the notator to the company. Always maintaining a low profile, he worked steadily throughout the war years, notating in great detail a ballet a year and improving the manuscript of his *Handbook*. At first it was handwritten with carbon copies but even though the war was still going on, he managed to find a small offset printer who would make him 120 copies.

Towards the end of the war, Knust again found himself without paid employment, so once more he devoted time to writing his eight-volume *Encyclopedia of Kinetography*. This was published after the war and in time for Laban to receive a copy for his seventieth birthday in 1948. Laban may not have been too willing to acknowledge it, but by this time Knust knew more about the method of notation than the master who formulated the script.

Then, in 1950, when Laban produced his *Mastery of Movement on the Stage*, he felt justified in incorporating 50 movements from Knust's book, with acknowledgement. Knust, however, never felt that this inclusion was appropriate since he saw them not as movement examples but explanations of the rules of dance script.

During the war years, the use of notation had been developing in England and the Laban Notation Bureau had been set up in New York. But, like any language or means of recording it, variations and deviations soon became evident. At first, there was a good deal of debate and even infighting as to whose approach was 'right'. When Laban died in 1958, it was evident that there was a need to find a means to end disputes, so the International Council of Kinetography Laban was formed, with Knust as its president.

Typically, he never used his position to assert his authority in these matters. While he was anxious to unite disparate ideas into a coherent system, he never saw diversity as anything but an opportunity for enrichment. He used his understanding, knowledge and clarity of thought and judgement to bring disparate approaches together into what became a stronger, more universal script. He continued to work diligently on Kinetographie Laban right through to his death at just over eighty in 1977. Unhappily, he did not live quite long enough to enjoy the publication of his *Dictionary of Kinetography Laban*. But Knust did complete it before his death and it stands as testimony to his generous and devoted life.

Lisa Ullmann

Amongst the Jooss Company working at Dartington when Laban arrived was a thirty-year-old teacher, Lisa Ullmann. Born in June 1907, she was the second child of a lawyer, Dr Alfred Ullmann, who was a keen amateur impressionist painter. Lisa was brought up in Berlin at 5 Ruckerstrasse, the family home that heaved with artistic activity, becoming a venue for all kinds of meetings, poetry-readings and rehearsals largely stimulated by her elder brother, Walter, an actor. When Lisa left school, it was her ambition, no doubt inspired by her father, to become a painter.

She enrolled for a number of courses at the Academy of Arts but her father was obviously keen for her to have a broad educational experience so she also attended the Laban School in Berlin, which had been run by Hertha Feist since the autumn of 1922.

She enrolled on the layman's course and joined the movement choir. Laban came from time to time, mainly to examine and meet the students and it was on one of these visits that Lisa first heard him talk. At that point she was not greatly impressed by the maestro. She admitted 'everything seemed rather awesome to me and I don't think I understood much of what it was all about.' Yet it was a start and something in what Laban said evoked at least 'a sympathetic response'.[27]

Her tutors saw in Lisa a promising teacher with undoubted movement aptitude and talked her into suspending her studies at the Academy of Arts in favour of full-time training in movement. There was, however, something about Hertha Feist that did not quite click with Lisa, so she joined the other Laban School in Berlin, run by Lotte Wedekind, niece of Frank Wedekind, the expressionist playwright. Here Lisa, still keeping her options open, joined the certificate course for prospective teachers of dance and took the qualifying exams in front of Laban in the summer of 1927.

For a further two years, she stayed on, teaching and studying for the much coveted Laban Diploma. Towards the end of that time, Laban himself gave a four-week intensive course to the candidates. It was this experience which finally determined Lisa to give up her aspirations to paint in favour of full-time teaching of movement and dance. She obtained her diploma and began to look for work.

Not long after, Kurt Jooss was looking for an additional teacher to work with his school and company and invited Lisa Ullmann to Essen to join his staff, which she did early in 1930. Then, when the company moved to Dartington in 1934, Lisa accompanied them. For Jooss, she was only an average teacher.

When Laban arrived in 1938, he did not want to see anybody (or any bodies). Gradually, as his health improved, he began to see a few visitors amongst whom was the young teacher of the second-year students, Lisa Ullmann, who, like Jooss, could at least converse with him in German. Like so many people before and since, Lisa gradually came under Laban's charismatic aura and devotedly went to see him whenever she had time free from her teaching.

Then war broke out and the next major change in Laban's life took place in June 1940. Jooss and Leeder were interned as aliens. The Ballet Jooss was disbanded. Wartime regulations would not allow German nationals to remain within three miles of the coast, so the Elmhirsts, who had first invited Jooss and his ballet company to Devon, offered Laban and Lisa their London flat in Baker Street.

Lisa began to see it as her task to look after Laban. With the best of intentions, from this point on she became his protector, his public relations officer seeking to re-establish Laban and his reputation in England. But she never really understood Laban the artist – it was the teacher in her that took over and a teacher newly inspired by the man she now sought to promote.

The Blitz soon followed and they had to evacuate to Newtown in Wales. None of Laban's recent experiences gave him optimism. In Britain, at war with Germany from which he had so recently escaped, there was no easy route back to eminence, authority and respect. He neither understood nor spoke English except in the most halting fashion.

Since his treatment by the Nazis he had come to hate human physicality, and in any case the war suspended the work of most ballet companies. Theatres were, for the most part, closed. Laban became a recluse.

If the odds had been against Laban while he was under house arrest in Schloss Banz, Germany, after the 1936 Olympic Games, they must have seemed almost worse now, four years later, isolated in rural Wales. How could a ballet-master from Berlin possibly survive in enemy territory in Newtown, Powys?

Once again, Laban had come across another saviour. According to several accounts, Laban was not so keen on Lisa as he had been on many of his former female associates and companions but she had qualities that he was to grow to appreciate. She was alert, energetic, determined, responsive. She had a good grasp of English and a sound enough grasp of several aspects of Laban theory to be able to put them to practical use. She was still young enough to be enthusiastic about life even in the face of great odds, yet knowing enough to be able to see ways of turning enthusiasm into tangible reality. The odds did seem stacked against them – a native and a naturalized German seeking to earn a living in the land of their country's most bitter enemy.

Lisa became a lively and dynamic teacher and her belief in and dedication to Laban took hold. She cycled alone through the Welsh countryside in search of commissions for Laban and herself and in doing so she fostered a remarkable change in Laban's life, work and influence. Could either of them have realized that this struggle would also be the beginning of new developments in the application of Laban's work?

Joan Littlewood, who had many heart-to-hearts with Laban in her Manchester days during the war, maintains in *Joan's Book* that Lisa 'sidetracked him into education' and that she 'wanted acceptance by the Education Authorities, a steady income, a regular life – and for him no temptations.'

At least the last part is true, for Lisa did not want anyone to take him away from her. Lisa did not 'know' Laban's previous involvement with theatre. Her training was that of a teacher and education was where she felt secure, so not surprisingly that was where she made her contacts.

Laban's previous preoccupation with dance – with concepts like the 'World of the Dancer', with his *A Life for Dance*, with the theatre – now became translated into the idea of Movement for Life, a life dedicated to the ramifications of movement, all on a broader, wider scale. Even his Kinetographie Laban became less the dancer's script and more the means of writing down and accounting for any form of human movement.

Clearly the route into education was not just Lisa's quest for security. It was also the force of circumstances. War is a time for adaptation and concentration on essentials. Unfortunately, no one in times of conflict wants to know about creative expression; they want what will help the war effort. Lisa (and she involved Laban in this) was prepared to face the wartime need for everyone to keep fit. So evening and weekend courses were begun.

People were quick to appreciate that the Laban approach to physical fitness was very different from anything Britain had seen before. There had been a little Laban-inspired dance teaching prior to the war but now a larger population was able to experience him in a general way. Those who attended his classes did not need further persuasion. News spread and the work began to extend throughout the country into all levels of the educational system.

Laban theory was there and only needed some rethinking, adaptation and extension. Laban began to enjoy this challenge. The new partnership worked effectively. Laban was the innovative theorist; Lisa was the invigorating and inspiring teacher. She had a way of inspiring all her classes with zeal. 'After each lesson,' Veronica Sherborne wrote in her Bedford College diary in 1941, 'as well as feeling physically exhilarated, one feels mentally uplifted as though one has done something of great importance, or had a glimpse of a world one only reads about.'[28]

When a book on *Modern Educational Dance* was called for, the name on the cover was Rudolf Laban but the text was largely Lisa's adaptation of his theory. Laban acknowledged this in a letter to Suzanne Perrottet, when he said that the *Modern Educational Dance* work was mostly Lisa's.

Suddenly there were calls for Laban to work in industry (largely through Paton Lawrence and Co.), in what was then called 'time and motion' studies; there were calls for help in training actors, both amateur and professional (mainly through the British Drama League and Northern Theatre School), and for explorations into movement therapy (mainly through Withymead Centre for psychotherapy). At every stage, Lisa was the organizer of these new initiatives and when Laban was too busy or too ill to meet these new demands, Lisa, in discussion with him, found the most appropriate substitute.

By 1946 Laban's work had become established enough in England to think in more permanent terms again, to consider setting up a studio to act as headquarters and serve as a base for full-time courses in Laban's method. Wartime had moved most things out of London and much Laban activity had centred round Manchester, so that was where Lisa Ullmann first established her Art of Movement Studio; for it was hers and Laban, at this stage, only acted as a faculty figure within the organization.

Lisa had unflagging energy and drive, which was reflected in the steady growth of student enrolment at the Art of Movement Studio and the steady proliferation of short courses and single sessions which were run under her auspices. In just two years (by September 1948), Lisa had won Ministry of Education approval for her one-year course for teachers, an achievement which put the studio on a much sounder financial base.

In August 1953, the Laban Art Of Movement Studio moved to Woburn Hill, Addlestone, in Surrey, into premises donated by William Elmhirst, the son of the founder of Dartington Hall Trust. This marked an important move to permanent country premises where Laban ideas and ideals might be practised.

Lisa was the principal of the Studio and while she built most things around Laban, she did tend to overprotect him, almost regarding him, like the studio, as hers. She kept tight reins on all that went on in the studio and remained jealous of anyone whom she felt was getting close to Laban or might be veering away towards too much independence with the work.

So while it seems wholly unlikely that Laban's work would have found such a broad revival in England through the efforts and energies of Lisa Ullmann it did. It is also evident, however, that she did not possess Laban's breadth of vision, nor seem concerned that he re-establish his place in dance theatre. It took a new principal to reinstate the dance training and performance around the name of Laban.

After Laban's death, Lisa continued to direct activities at the studio very much along the same lines as before, focusing primarily on educational dance training. She continued her position until 1972, when the Trust provided her with a house and a pension which enabled her to continue her role as guardian of Laban ideas and interpretation. Until her death in 1985, she remained in charge of all Laban's books and manuscripts, publishing some materials, editing and re-editing others in an attempt to make them more accessible. She would no doubt have thought it appropriate that she came to the end of her life at the same age as Laban came to the end of his.

Part Three
LABAN'S DOCUMENTED IDEAS

'. . . it may make take fifty years but people will find out and be interested in what Laban did, saw and wrote . . .'

Joseph Lewitan

Laban's Documented Ideas

Laban's Writing: Its Purpose and Context

So far, we have considered what might be seen as circumstantial evidence in the understanding of Laban. Now it is time to examine the documentary material to ascertain what Laban himself records of his ideas. Laban wrote dozens of articles and published ten books. The frustration we encounter lies in the fact that he never actually devoted a single volume to clarifying his all-encompassing philosophy or even the basic principles which underlie it. Several people asked him to undertake such a task but he always refused.

Jooss says that in the early 1920s, while he himself wanted everything cut and dried, Laban was not interested in formulating a clear theory. Jooss even went to Laban for 'a system' but the master brushed his suggestion aside. Laban explained he did not want a system because firstly there would have to be too many exceptions and exemptions, and secondly his theory was still evolving, always changing. Laban's point was that he was 'thinking about life and life is never exact. Life is free.'[1]

In any case, Laban himself was acutely aware of the peril of setting any of his ideas down on the page. It seems he remained dissatisfied with all the books he had written. In 1954 he told Yat Malmgren that, at times, he wished he had not written them but had felt obliged to respond to the need that had been created. It was as specific requests expressed themselves that Laban wrote books and articles. These usually indicated how his ideas might work out in relation to this or that activity and generally in response to an immediate specific approach. Someone wanted a book about gymnastics or educational dance, or an article about notation or some aspect of the new ballet – and so he wrote to fulfil a pressing need. His first and fifth books are interesting exceptions: the first (*The Dancer's World*) presents Laban's overview of the dancer and his role in his world and the other (*A Life for Dance*) is an impressionistic view of Laban's own role in his world – his life. So it is crucial to examine each of his major publications to clarify their contents; we can appreciate the value of each if we consider them in context.

The first volume in German was published two years after the end of the First World War. His first volume in English was published two years after the Second World War. Dates given are those of publication, so it is as well to remember that the ideas predate those years.

The five German editions were published during the fifteen years betwen 1920 and 1935, when Laban was between the ages of forty and fifty-five. The five books in English appeared during the last ten years of his life (between the ages of sixty-nine and seventy-nine). One other volume, *Choreutics*, was published in 1966, eight years after his death, but it really belongs to the period just before the Second World War or earlier.

8 The Context and Content of Laban's Main Works in German

The Dancer's World

Laban's first book, *Die Welt des Tänzers* [The Dancer's World] (1920), was published in Stuttgart by Walter Seifert Verlag. Laban had been involved in dance work, both in theory and practice, for almost ten years. Articles had been written about him and he had published two or three himself, notably in the periodical *Die Tat*. He had been operating before the war in Munich and Ascona; then, during the period of hostilities, his work was mainly centred on Zurich. With the return of peace, publishers began to seek new work and Laban was invited to write something. He already had a growing reputation and a book in print would undoubtedly enhance his standing and, he hoped, have a positive effect on the status of the dance in general.

This book sets the tone and pattern of his early thinking in many ways. It was written for that special between-the-wars artistic German public who were attuned to mysticism and romanticism. It is a book for his contemporaries involved in the dance and, he explains, is to be read as a poetic exploration rather than a practically oriented volume. He acknowledges at the outset that he is setting himself an impossible task in trying to write at all about dance and movement – to put into words something that by its very nature defies words. Yet he wants to reach out and 'gain as wide an understanding as possible'.[2]

Years later, when Laban reflected on this work, he expressed his dissatisfaction with it to Lisa Ullmann and told her how he had assembled the material. The inveterate note-maker had set out his papers all over the floor and put them into order by prodding them onto a stick with a nail at the end. True to form, these were shaped intuitively into a number of sections which grouped his responses. It should not be surprising, then, to encounter a range of approaches. The language is at times metaphorical, sometimes fanciful and florid; on other occasions, it is positively evangelical and mystical.

Appropriately, Laban found a justification and a meta-phor in the dance itself:

> The purest image of the dance of dances . . . is the round which vibrates the whole of the human body.

So he skilfully defended his format by setting his ideas out, not in the usual structure of paragraphs and chapters but by putting his ideas down as a series of 'thought rounds'.

It is meant to be an awakening of insight into dance and was designed 'before publishing the "Dancer's Script" to give a clear indication of *the essence of dance and the dancer*'. It is not, Laban hastens to explain, 'a book about exercises and techniques, but an explanation of ideas which form the ethics and moral attitude of the dance from which the techniques and theories follow'.[3]

This work of 264 quarto pages has a number of aims and aspirations. Laban was anxious to set dance up as an art form of value and on equal footing with the other arts. Dance and ballet in Germany before and after the First World War were still at a low ebb artistically and Laban wanted to challenge the view that dance was empty and fanciful. Instead, he pointed to the 'inherent cultural forces in the art of dancing and dance practice'. Laban's book is as basic to the dance as, say, Aristotle's *Poetics* is to the drama. Similarly it is at one and the same time just about as stimulating and, in being 'essence', as frustrating.

The subtitle of the book is *Fünf Gedankenreigen* – 'five dances of thought' – so it is divided into five sections with an overall introduction. Every round is a series of grouped sentences or phrases, each with a subheading, containing a series of related (though not necessarily logical) ideas – like beads on a string – juxtaposed though not interwoven.

Summary of Content

Foreword

Laban sets out to challenge preconceived notions of dance and dancers. At the basis is a refutation that life is chaos and confusion but he maintains that real dancers hope to communicate a sense of purpose and destiny for the human race.

He hopes to kindle an awareness of the interrelationship between the limbs and the harmoniously balanced whole person and states that dance is rooted in the whole personality. Within man is the dance of the earth which uses at the core of its expression the force of *tension*. This tension is the basis of all change; it is through the play of tension that we experience the sense of time, space and dynamic.

Laban identifies two of his chief influences: Plato, who he says 'in the *Timaeus*, has passed on Pythagoras's cosmology which is a kind of declaration of faith of the dancer'; and the dervishes, because 'in Sufism is expressed something of this universal occurrence when they talk about the "dance of the spheres around god".'

Round I

Forms of Human Expression: Laban enters Delsartian territory here, considering physical, emotional, vocal and intellectual expressions and communication. He talks about their relationship to harmony and balance, to tension and relaxation; the place of tension in all forms of expression: intellectual, emotional and physical; the value of analysis of physical direction, energy applied and duration of time taken. The four main directions start from the body's centre of gravity. The place of dance in helping the dancer come closer to the unity and meaning of things. The need for further research and scientific dance investigation.

Round II

The Dancer and his Instrument: a detailed consideration of the physical and spiritual make-up of the body and its relation to the world around. Dance in all things: in man, in crystal, in plant and animal. Gravitational pull and the dancer's use of tension and relaxation in the service of dance expression. Spatial laws of eurhythmics in gestural variations. Physical intelligence; the importance of breathing in developing expressive power; the communication of the dancer's understanding.

Round III

Dance as Education: a consideration of the purpose and function of dance in a number of historical contexts: religious, mystical, social rites and rituals. Value today of those who understand movement, its use in therapy, physical development and spiritual awareness. Value of festival. The need for a life rhythm with its effort and recovery. Rhythm in all aspects of life and the understanding of this rhythmic pattern as a means of restoring and maintaining harmony and balance. Different kinds of dance and their functions. The importance of body sense and dance education.

Round IV

Dance as Art: characterized by the dedication of the artist to the values of the dance; an artist is concerned with self-denial, not self-display. Consideration of a variety of approaches to the work of art: pictorialism, impressionism, expressionism and some of the processes and elements which are involved in the creative expression of a composition together with its artistic communication. Recording this dance work through a dance script.

Round V

Aesthetics of Dance: number, form – linear, faceted or plastic, kinds and forms of dance, music, symbol, colour, light, mood. Analysis of movement, tension and balance. Dance and movement in the whole pattern of things.

Afterword

Tributes paid to, and surveys of, the work of forerunners and fellow workers. There is a bibliography which covers historic and contemporary texts on dancing (Noverre through to Brandenburg), works on Anatomy, Notation, Physiology, Psychology and Crystallography.

All Laban's basic ideas are touched on in this book. Here are his initial statements about any number of topics that continued to occupy his investigation: tension and relaxation, harmony and balance, rhythm, effort and recovery. He talks about space and direction in space, energy applied (weight) and duration of time. He considers the body in detail and points out the importance of breathing in expression. He relates human movement to plant, animal and crystal. He claims a central position for dance throughout life – in rituals (religious and social) as well as indicating its value in therapy. This is the only one of all Laban's writings to contain a reading list.

In its day *The Dancer's World* was a challenge to new thinking about dance, its nature and function, and even now it remains important as an overview of Laban's holistic philosophy of dance. As a kind of ABC of dance theory, it is a book to be referred to rather than read, and its ideas need to be pondered over. Some of the material comes over as perceptive, even profound; some of it seems more commonplace. Some sections seem at one reading profound, at another commonplace. Irmgard Bartenieff, who worked with Laban in the 1920s, points out that, 'In spite of all, it was an important book. In its day it served to draw many dancers to him and enhanced his reputation.'[4]

Laban wrote a number of articles following this (developing further ideas on dance and dance theatre), but it was not until 1926 that his next books appeared and then no fewer than three in that one year. And that, in any case, was quite a year for Laban.

Children's Dance and Gymnastics

Des Kindes Gymnastik und Tanz [*Children's Gymnastics and Dance*], (1926) appeared first, just prior to the companion book written about adult dance education – both concerning the application of his work in the field of recreation. The previous years, following the publication of *The Dancer's World*, were those in which Laban's activity had been hectic if not feverish. There were tours of his full company, tours of the chamber group and tours of Laban with Loeszer. The non-professional work had been growing especially under fellow workers like Martin Gleisner and Albrecht Knust and the two books on gymnastics and dance were a result of the need expressed by teachers and other educators for further guidance.

This book of 134 pages (together with 38 photographic illustrations of pupils from various Laban schools) has no chapter divisions and no headings of any kind. The construction of many of the sentences is complicated and often confusing. Many of its paragraphs are extremely long, adding further difficulty to keeping track of the shape of the discussion. It is, overall, a very discursive treatise, setting out a broad (rather romantic) educational philosophy, examining the place of gymnastics in the life of the growing child.

Summary of Content

The models for the form of gymnastic exercises and training should, Laban argues, be drawn from those physical activities that children most naturally engage in: free, flowing, rhythmic and often accompanied by sounds which the child him/herself makes. Laban outlines what he sees as three life periods in the developing child (to be covered by this book): the period of natural experiencing of the world outside is followed by the period at school when understanding and knowledge are developed and when introspection is encouraged. The third stage he identifies as that from adolescence to coming-of-age, when further bodily changes are accompanied by a sense of curiosity and adventure once more. In his own way, Laban outlines the development of the child's expressiveness along lines similar to those of Delsarte.

The new gymnastics is not to be confused with apparatus skill or with other arts. It is neither a game nor an art. It is concerned with freedom of expression; it is dance with an educational purpose. The expressive is as important as the exercise aspect. Its objects are:

> good posture
> strengthening the body
> confidence and command of space
> knowledge and command of rhythmic laws
> general fitness
> release of creativity.

These objects are achieved by body training through

performing movement sequences exploring different directions and muscle tensions. From this, an expressive alphabet is built up (as we might employ words and sentences) without it becoming a complete composition or a work of art. The child is not burdened with detailed theory of space harmony but through experience can begin to sense this reality. Laban does, however, maintain that children should, at an early age, be taught movement notation rather as they are given access to musical notation.

Gymnastics should give the child physical freedom and lead to a harmonious development of the whole person; freeing the body leads to enriching of the mind and spirit. At the basis of the approach is breathing and sound, tone and noise are audible movements. Rhythm and harmony can arise from natural and imaginative exercises. Group work and dramatic play as well as choreographic play can help to strengthen and develop the body and the child's social awareness.

From time to time, Laban makes reference to the mathematical basis of dance and gymnastics, and points to links between the centre of gravity in the body and the earth's axis. He draws attention to the angles of the diagonals in space and points out that 'these two angles, as distinct from the dimensional space cross, have a ratio between them which is very close to the Golden Section'. This ratio 'appears to be the ratio which gives us the feeling of a beautiful and harmonious movement'. So, he claims, pleasure and power can lead to greater expression and even spiritual experience.

Laban advocates the use of the movement choir which can aid confidence besides being able to 'strengthen and fulfil the individual's focus and development'. Much of the work, he maintains, should be dramatic, declaring that 'a kind of acting and pantomime must form the base.'

There is an interesting discussion of the way the child

employs grotesque and caricature, so utilizing tension freely to lead to relaxation: 'Afterwards, he breathes freely with renewed pleasure and agility'.[5]

Throughout the book, Laban seems to be recalling aspects of his own childhood and pleading for free play as the way of maintaining the healthy balance with which young people are naturally endowed. It is a pity that the book is not easy to read in all parts, since the ideas throughout still seem to make educational sense. Here is Laban thinking more specifically about applying his ideas to the growing child. He wants them actively and imaginatively involved (based on sound movement principles) rather than bogged down with theory.

Gymnastics and Dance

In *Gymnastik und Tanz* [*Gymnastics and Dance*] (1926), Laban considers the adult problems and the need for all to 'learn, use, see and understand their bodies'. Once man has this knowledge, he argues, his former longing for, and present fulfilment of, the rhythmic will establish itself with such strength that he will want to express himself through the basic elements of dancing.

This text has 179 pages with 54 photographs. The photographs of solo and group dancers are intended to illuminate the ideas of the text; the mood in these strongly dynamic poses is highly expressionist throughout.

Summary of Content

Chapter 1: The Basic Fundamental Ideas of Gymnastics

In which Laban faces why man used gymnastics in the past and man's present needs. The mastery of the 'choreological laws of space' is emphasized in a general way though their exact nature is not discussed.

Chapter 2: Movement Culture and a view of its place in the world

The benefits that can accrue from gymnastics – physically, spiritually and morally. Again, he talks of this being the power we are looking for and reminds us that it was known in antiquity.

Chapter 3: Anatomy as a Basis for the Laws of Movement

The laws of space in the icosahedron; harmony, scales, exercises for breathing and therapy.

Chapter 4: Social Possibilities

With special reference to movement choirs. Considers various physical activities but finds sport wanting in its one-sidedness. Again he looks to the ancient Greek ideal.

Chapter 5: The Art of Movement

Including an examination of the art of dancing in comparison to gymnastics and historic dance. Dance comes out best as it brings man in touch with his religious and spiritual side.

Chapter 6: Conclusion

Dance helps to relate man to the rhythm and forces of nature.

He begins on a sound premise, that everyone needs to understand and use their bodies, but does not follow this ideal logically through. *Children's Gymnastics and Dance* covered some of the ground, so here he is looking for other things to say and too often takes refuge in the historical view. Both books contain elements of Laban's approach to space harmony more from the philosophic point of view than the abstract and geometric.

Choreography

The publication of *Choreographie* [*Choreography*] (1926) was simultaneous with the founding of the Choreographic Institute in Würzburg. The institute had a special aim, which was to develop the study of choreology and the writing of dance as an aid to composition.

Choreography is largely technical in its follow-on from *Gymnastics and Dance*. In the amply illustrated (with photographs but mainly symbols and diagrams) 103-page booklet, Laban examines the 'dynamic theory of forms', looking in more detail at technical ideas he had mentioned in earlier works.

Summary of Content

The book consists of classifications and technical explanations of various sequences of movement. He explains his thinking and suggests a number of solutions to notation problems. Laban maintains that there are 'plastic and balancing tensions in space' which are governed by a law and it is this law that choreographic investigation sets out to eliminate.

The theory of the twelve directions in space is outlined and illustrated by referring to classical ballet and fencing positions which are placed within the icosahedron. Twelve of the illustrations show individuals inside a full-sized model of an icosahedron with limbs outstretched towards the outer surfaces of the shape. Aspects of rhythm, space tensions, balance, stability and dynamic quality are also considered. The movement sequences are outlined in some detail, together with their dynamic value, most supported by diagrams and symbols.

This was the first official publication of his symbols for dance notation, which were later developed into 'Kinetographie Laban'.

Between May and July of that year he was touring the USA, lecturing and studying. He wrote other articles on such topics as *The Dance Theatre* and *The Idea of Movement Choirs*. By the summer of the following year (1927), the Choreographic Institute had moved to Berlin and Laban had organized the first ever gathering of professionals involved with dance at the First Dancers' Congress in Magdeburg.

A year later still, in 1928, Laban had founded the German Society for Dance Writing with its journal *Schrifttanz* (edited by Alfred Schlee of Universal Editions). This was the first magazine in which various aspects of dance writing could be discussed as well as dance theory, aesthetics and history. Writers from many dance areas contributed, though much of it focused round Laban's work and Laban himself wrote a number of the articles.

The Second Dancers' Congress was held in Essen that year, and there Laban presented his kinetographic system. Laban and his fellow workers had for years been developing the signs for a dance script which would enable all and any human activity to be recorded. The congress decided to adopt Laban's approach as the main notation for stage dance. Now as well as being able to write about dance, dance itself could be written.

Subsequent articles focused largely on dance notation and some of the problems of dance writing. Once Hitler took power, there was a notable emergence of writing which uses the adjective *Deutsche* (German) when talking about dance and suggests that Germany was the country in which Dance Theatre had its first and deepest roots. Laban the one-time internationalist seemed to be narrowing his own ideals.

In 1933, *Schrifttanz* was taken over and incorporated into *Der Tanz*. It was not until 1935 that Laban published his next book and the last one he wrote in the German language. So far it had been the theory that had claimed his attention in writing. Now he turned to his life, which he proclaimed was *A Life for Dance* (1935). When he had reached the age of fifty in 1929, there had been considerable interest shown in the progress of the man behind the theory. In recent years he had become still further renowned, having designed and directed the Vienna Festival celebrations (1929), choreographed at the Bayreuth Wagner Festival (1930 and 1931), been appointed ballet-master to the Berlin State Opera (1930–34), and become Director for the German Dance Theatre (1934–36).

A Life for Dance

Ein Leben für den Tanz [*A Life for Dance*] (1935) is not so much an autobiography as a testimonial-cum-dance-drama based on events which took place in his life. It stands at the opposite end of the spectrum from *The Dancer's World*. Whereas *The Dancer's World* was the more abstract approach to writing about ideas on dance, *A Life for Dance* is more of the myth and legend approach which communicates artistic rather than documentary facts.

The book is 226 pages long and includes nine black-and-white line drawings executed by Laban, illustrating different aspects of themes of the text. It is divided into three sections, broadly grouping his reminiscences – influences and impressions of early childhood and youth; consolidation and spread of theory; and wider application of his ideas.

There are chapters within these sections: most of these chapters are given a heading which is the title of a dance. So although the book does not give any clear indication of his chronological biography, it does indicate the close links between his life and his dance creativity. Material within each of the eleven chapters can often be related to different periods within his life. Patience is required, as it becomes like playing some detective game as references jump backwards and forwards in years, none of which is specifically referred to. More often than not, Laban is at pains to disguise names and places, at best referring to them by a single initial. Lisa Ullmann in her version of the work in English (1975) has dated some of the events and annotated others.

In general, however, it is possible to relate each chapter (roughly) to one part of his life more than another.

Summary of Content

Part I

Chapter 1: The Fool's Mirror – early childhood.
Chapter 2: The Earth – travels with his father.
Chapter 3: The Night – the Paris years.
Chapter 4: The Sorcerer's Apprentice – army training.
Chapter 5: The Tiger – a period in Nice.
Chapter 6: The Fiddler – romance in northern Hanover.

Part II

Chapter 1: The Swinging Temple – early festivals.
Chapter 2: Illusions – Hamburg years.
Chapter 3: The Titan – tour in USA.

Part III

Chapter 1: Everyday Life and Festival – festivals between the war.
Chapter 2: Roads to the Future – dance and drama notations for all occasions.

To appreciate the book, it is best to read it for broad insight and understanding of some roots of Laban's ideas and their expression through his dance-dramas. This is the romantic

Laban – romantic in the sense that he is weaving a fantasy, a picturesque fairy-tale, or an exaggerated, imaginative narrative based on fact.

It is interesting that Laban should be writing in this escapist way at a time when all around him were the horrors of the Nazi regime. A stringent artistic clamp-down followed the burning of books in 1933 after Hitler became Chancellor. The following year, when Laban must have been writing (or dictating) *A Life*, was the year that Jooss had fled with his company just in time to escape Nazi persecution and almost all the eminent German writers, musicians and artists were emigrating. All Jewish producers, directors and actors who could, left the country.

Every manuscript of a book had to be submitted to the Propaganda Ministry for approval before publication. Frau Marie Luise Lieschke was working closely with Laban at the time and seems to have been especially facilitating in matters to do with the official Nazi party negotiations. She was writing a good many of his business letters and those which she sent out under Laban's name always carry the offical concluding salutation of the time – *Heil Hitler*. Laban might have been politically naïve, but Lieschke knew the importance of not putting a foot wrong.

Some, notably Gleisner and Jooss, detected passages in the book which might be said to be placatory or written with the Nazis in mind. Gleisner, in two interviews given long after, remained worried that his, Gleisner's, German text quoted in Part II had, he said, been expurgated: instead of ending 'love, kin, country, and mankind', it finished, he maintained, with only 'love, kin, country', leaving out Gleisner's concern for the brotherhood of all mankind.[6]

There are certainly passages (that strike one as foreign to Laban's outlook) which seem to praise the soldier and emphasize the glory of army comradeship alongside 'all-embracing unity to the fatherland'. Yet equally, other sections stand as a direct challenge to this. Laban recalls a conversation that he had with a colleague in Nice: 'an artist who has noble feelings should not go along with the falsehoods and deceptions of his time. It is essential that we should aspire to be angels, even if they can never reach those heights.' Taken all in all, the book is far too fanciful and romantic to be seen as a work going very far beyond his stated purpose of showing 'the whole kaleidoscope of events' in a life 'devoted to his art', resulting in a 'round of events and thoughts in which various threads are interwoven'. It is a series of free-associations around periods and themes of his life through to the end of the 1920s. It may be significant that *A Life* stops short of the Nazi period, for he makes no reference to or commentary on events much after 1930.

A Life for Dance marks the beginning of the period of the great divide. Laban did not publish another book until 1948, by which time he was in Britain and the war with Germany was over. There were, however, two fairly substantial pieces of writing which he undertook between those years: the first he wrote in Germany while he was in Schloss Banz, the other was in England while he was trying to recover from his disillusionment, just before war was declared on the Germany he had so recently left.

A Statement on the Setting up of the German Dance Theatre (1937, unpublished)

Laban was not about to give up his life's work easily. Even though Hitler had removed him from his job as Director for Dance, cancelled his Olympic Games performance, forbidden his name or books to be used and placed him in house arrest in a disused monastery in Schloss Banz, it seems he still found it difficult to accept that he might not still recoup his losses. Almost alone, he began writing and attempting to present a case for German Dance Theatre.

Summary of Content

Laban's main thrust in these 60 typed pages of manuscript is that there is a future for dance in Germany. Although dance has been treated as a Cinderella, it is, he claims, unlike the other arts since it is plastic and self-expressive in a way that they are not. It is the original art form out of which the other arts have grown and is capable of expressing things which cannot be expressed in other art forms. It will reveal all kinds and sides of individuality though it will not always work in terms of a logical series of events. Dance itself can find expression in variety and diversity. It can be historical, of the recent past, of the present or even the future. It can be lyrical, dramatic, epic: it can accommodate all kinds and shapes of people, from 'high' dancers to 'low' or 'deep' dancers. Dance refreshes the reserves of energy and should not be regarded as dangerous. It calls for team spirit and can emphasize nationalism.

The other arts have their specialized venues and dance needs its 'Dome' where as this plastic art it can be fully appreciated. This is a chance for Laban in some detail to outline his cherished ideas on the form of the ideal dance amphitheatre which could also be used for festivities and other massed gatherings. He discusses what dance needs in terms of performer–spectator relationship and stresses again that dance will not flourish without its own space to call home. (An Appendix includes nine sketches illustrating the primary requirements.)

Dance can work with the other arts, but not as a subordinate. On the contrary, other arts can serve the dance but should be employed to bring out its three-dimensional form and relate to its rhythm. Dance is an art form in its own right and needs to be liberated from opera. Laban points out that three main forms of dance exist: the professional and 'art' dance, the community dance with its moving chorus, and what he calls society dance – akin to parades. In spite of the reawakening in Germany of the striving for physical culture, Laban maintains that the goal of spiritual resurgence will not be reached without dance. It is in sections like this that he seems most aware of the Nazi authorities, arguing that, 'dance has what you want'. It has cultural value for the new age.

In discussing various styles of dance, he identifies four main groups and goes out of his way to argue that certain styles associated with negro forms are really not so in origin but have been taken by the negroes from Scotland, northern Europe and elsewhere.

Not surprisingly, he includes a strong plea for recording dance through its own notation, giving it status alongside those other arts where a script already exists. In *A Life for Dance* he had declared dance to be 'an art which cannot be caught and canned by machine', but in this statement (a mere two years later) he has altered his view and sees that film has a role in recording dance alongside notation. There is also now, in his view, a place for dance on film, especially when it is expressionistic. It is a somewhat long, rambling and repetitious document going over well-tried themes and theories, pushing certain aspects of German nationalism and finally sounding like his last-ditch attempt to give dance its pride of place in German culture. But it failed to persuade anyone. It was, however, to prove his last major written piece on dance. A year later, Laban was in Dartington Hall, a sick man of almost sixty. When he arrived in England, all he had of his work was what he could carry in his head. But his first call was health, of both mind and body, not work. He needed to rest and seek remedies. Jooss set him up in the summerhouse where he seemed to find solace and therapy constructing abstract geometric shapes.

9 The Context and Content of Laban's Main Works in English

The move to England and English marks a sharp contrast in the content of his writing. Laban first undertook the task of writing about 'the basic trends of his thought'. In his then current frame of mind, he selected the most abstract aspect of his theory – what he chose to call 'choreutics', the art or science dealing with the analysis and synthesis of movement.

Choreutics

The general idea was to make some of his discoveries available to the English public; not surprisingly, since he knew very little English, they turned out to be presented in a very technical, mathematical way. Since he had at that time no means of income, there might also have been a hope of deriving something from publication. There was then the problem of finding a publisher.

Lisa Ullmann, in her Preface to *Choreutics* (published by Macdonald and Evans, 1966), points out 'There was also the seemingly insurmountable problem of language'. In the almost twenty years that Laban spent in England, English could never be held to be a fluent means of expression for him, so one year after arrival the task of translating his ideas into English that read like English must have been a complicated one. However, Louise Soelberg, former Dance Director at Dartington, then with Jooss's company, came to the rescue and worked with Laban to lend the manuscript 'some degree of comprehensibility'.[7]

As far as Laban was concerned, this work was completed in June 1940, just as it was decreed that anyone of German nationality could no longer remain anywhere within three miles of the coast. Laban and Lisa left first for London, then moved to Wales. It was not until after Laban's death that Lisa Ullmann determined to seek publication and, with the help, this time, of Betty Redfern, edited the text.

Amongst the materials in her collection of Laban papers, Lisa Ullmann also had what she saw as a related work, presented to Laban on his fiftieth birthday in 1929. This had been compiled by Gertrude Snell, as a summary of Laban's abstract theories to that date. With her mathematical interests, she had worked alongside Laban over a number of years. Lisa decided to make this material Part II of the book.

So *Choreutics*, published eight years after Laban's death, really belongs to the between-the-wars period of his activities, being (a) Snell's 1929 summary of his abstract theory, the mathematics of movement, and (b) Laban's 1938 translated and edited summary of his approach to movement in the abstract, or movement in relation to geometric form. All these basic, abstract concepts, then, were completed before the Second World War. Laban appears not to have shown interest in publication of this work once he had reclaimed his interest and belief in people since there is no record of him having sought to retrieve it.

Although the word 'choreutics' is drawn from the idea of the 'wisdom of the circles', it is here extended to the 'study of various forms of harmonized movement', and concentrates on that aspect of Laban's work concerned primarily with the more abstract notions of space and the harmony of movement in space. This is in strong contrast to the *Statement* of two years earlier, where his interest was all on the dancer and the appropriate space in which to perform.

Part I (the Laban section) takes up 136 pages of this book of 210 pages in overall length. Ninety-seven diagram figures illustrate the text. Part I is divided into twelve short sections with an Introduction.

Summary of Content

The introduction, which still carries something of the 'thought round' approach, sets up the premise that movement, the basic and unifying experience of existence, only makes sense if it has an organic progress and is made up of moves in a natural progression. The aim is to analyse moves into a series of frames or stills (called here awkwardly 'standstills' and 'snapshots') which, joined together, follow a certain path or line ('pathways tracing shapes in space' – termed 'trace forms'). Movement sequences need a 'natural' order to maintain balance and harmony.

Chapter 1: Principles of Orientation in Space

Sets up the basics: terms such as the kinesphere, stance, direction, dimension, diametre, axes and levels and the Labanotation symbols that record them. Discussion of stance within the Kinesphere and the tracing of directions radiating from it.

Chapter 2: The Body and the Kinesphere

Establishes the points of reference for body movement, identifying the pentagon, the quadrangle and the tetrahedron as figures in relation to which it is possible to identify patterns and discover the movements said to be 'harmonious'. 'Laws' governing 'harmonious circles' are common to the human body and 'the whole of nature'.

Chapter 3: Exploration of the Dynasphere

Quality of movement and the feeling related to it are now

introduced, establishing, alongside the spatial form of the movement and inseparable from it, its energy or dynamic.

Chapter 4: Natural Sequences and Scales in Space

Harmonic movement is based on natural movement sequences (scales). Such activities as fencing, or swimming the crawl, link zones of the body together in a logical way. Also important is recognition of contrasting tensions – dimensional and diagonal – together with the overall economy of effort.

Chapter 5: The Body and Trace Forms

Every main movement is made up of myriad minor movements along its path; the legs take steps, the arms gather and scatter. Each of these is accompanied by feeling and so movement can be linked to spiritual awareness.

Chapter 6: Natural Sequences of the Dynasphere

The dynamics of each action have corresponding inner moods; some, closely associated (with easy transitions), some contrasting (with less smooth transitions). Combinations of the basic dynamic elements (speed, strength and direction) lead to the recognition of eight basic effort actions. The speed will vary from the fastest to the slowest; likewise, the strength will vary from very strong to weak while direction can be direct or indirect. Alongside these factors, our inner attitudes are often mirrored, in almost imperceptible movements, (often in hands and feet) known as 'shadow movements'. Though expression is personal, it is possible, through analysis, to become aware of the links between motion and emotion.

Chapter 7: The Standard Scale

The structure of the Kinesphere is first examined with its surface edges and its traversing lines – dimensions, diagonals, diametres and transversals, building to the twelve points of the 'scaffold'. The twelve linked movements which form sequences connecting these points (which can revolve around various axes), make up the primary scales and establish the basis for harmonic relations.

Chapter 8: Bodily Perspective

The shapes made in moving are built up from the four elements of straight, curved, twisted and rounded (which are also the basic lines from which most scripts are drawn). Movement is a means of putting us in touch with universals and enabling us to gain and sustain balance. The standard scale with its flow of forms is the basic experience of spatial harmony. All the expressions of movement, including 'shadow forms', lead towards an understanding of existence.

Chapter 9: The Stabilizing and Mobilizing of Trace Forms

Stability and mobility alternate endlessly; mobility brings a temporary loss of equilibrium; stability restores it. Movement is comprised of tension and release of tension, between inner and outer flux. Binding and loosening actions are found throughout the scales of the Dynasphere.

Chapter 10: Cubic and Spheric Forms of the Scaffold

The harmonic movement of human beings is of a fluid and curving nature, but the icosahedron, built up from the octahedron and the cube and which appears in structures such as crystals, seems a natural framework in which to study the movement of man. There are all kinds of interesting geometric proportions in the human body which link man with the universal and the infinite.

Chapter 11: Choreutic Shapes Performed by the Body

A well-balanced individual will find harmonies through natural expression, but restrictions for any reason (physical or psychological) are undesirable as it is important to be able to select from a full and complete range. Beginning with trace forms in the trunk and proceeding to free performance of choreutic shapes helps the integration of body and mind. There are strong links between the movement in all the arts but especially architecture and music, and a study of choreutics can lead to a more integrated understanding.

Chapter 12: Free Inclinations

The Kinesphere should not restrict but should free the movement and imagination. Free inclinations will have their starting point, deviation and end point but these indicate an infinite number of possible movements. All of these are capable of analysis through the understanding of structures and can add to the conscious enjoyment of movement experience.

Although presented in a largely mathematical form, this book does contain basic ideas of Laban theory especially as it relates to space and space harmony. It is abstract movement theory, almost entirely removed from people – 'the body' remains as abstract as 'the icosahedron'. Reference back to *The Dancer's World* will soon show the major change of approach but can also emphasize a through line of Laban ideas. Most concern here is with analysis and technical movement sequences as they relate to balance and harmony. Another important difference lies in the fact that it is no longer the dancer's world but the world for all movers. Whereas we could talk of *The Dancer's World* as being the

ABC of dance theory, *Choreutics* might be seen as a grammar for movement practice – as rudimentary and as dry.

From 1940 and Laban's wartime evacuation, until several years after Laban's death, the draft of *Choreutics* remained with Dorothy Elmhirst. Laban meanwhile answered other calls for his understanding. Wartime Britain had shortages of everything, including film, and it was this that first led the industrialist Frederic Charles Lawrence to Laban. Two years into the war, in 1941, whilst Laban and Lisa Ullmann were in Newtown in Wales, Lawrence heard about him and his work (especially his notation) from Bill Slater, the director of Dartington Hall Trust. Lawrence had expressed his disquiet at the work-study methods that were being employed by his firm. Bill Slater had obviously grasped something of Laban's philosophy and suggested that Lawrence should talk over his feelings with Laban.

The two finally met and from this it was agreed that Laban should visit Lawrence in Manchester, to see if he could aid a project with Tyresoles (Simon Engineering Company). This was to prove the beginning of a long, close association between the two men (and an even longer link with the Art of Movement Studio – through to the early 1970s, when Lawrence by that time was approaching eighty years of age). Lawrence was impressed by Laban's approach and found his notation and understanding of movement qualities invaluable in assessing all kinds of problems in industry.

Soon, Lisa Ullmann joined them on an ever-increasing number of visits to Manchester, Yorkshire and the Midlands. By 1942 they had launched the Laban/Lawrence Industrial Rhythm method and the work had grown so demanding that it was decided that Lisa and Laban should move to Manchester and set up an Art of Movement Studio.

Effort

Shortly after the end of the war, Lawrence had published a book on marginal costing with Macdonald and Evans and while visiting the publishers in this connection, asked them if they would be interested in printing a book by Rudolf Laban whose work he had talked about most enthusiastically. Armed with John Macdonald's interest, Lawrence returned to Laban suggesting that they write a book together. The details, and which aspects of the work would form the book, Lawrence left to Laban.

Throughout their working collaboration, Laban had, of course, made copious notes and for over two years worked with A. Proctor Burman (Lawrence's lifelong friend and associate) on appropriate terminology. Laban's English was still very limited, but his interest and struggle for perfection insatiable. He spent many hours with lexicology and told Lawrence that he found English much better to describe efforts than the German language. Lawrence was impressed at his pursuit of perfection in seeking the right word and thought of him as 'a tremendous dictionary eater'. They shared a common interest in 'human effort and the conviction that the study of effort is today necessary for everyone in his own personal life and in every field of activity in which he is engaged'.[8]

Effort was finally published in 1947 by Macdonald and Evans. Laban wrote the text, with Burman helping him refine the terms and technical aspects while Lawrence tidied the English. This was an opportunity for Laban to clarify, develop and apply some of his earlier theory and observations.

This 85-page book is divided into seven chapters with a preface. There are no illustrations, but actions referred to are given in the symbols of Labanotation.

Summary of Content

Preface

Few people are aware that what affects their happiness in work and life is the capacity to make the best use of their individual efforts. Up to now, concentration has been on the surface indication of effort rather than upon the effort itself. By combining their individual experiences in this area, Laban and Lawrence maintain they have been able both to save time in observation and to bring fresh insight into the very nature of effort itself. By employing the rhythms expressed in bodily action, they have been able to harness them as a training method tailored to individual needs. Once skilfully assessed, individual effort can be changed, improved and controlled by training. The discoveries made can be applied to all professions, not simply those within the industrial scene and can lead to increased enjoyment and efficiency.

Chapter 1: Economy of Human Effort

In industry we are faced with the challenge to unite man and the machine. This must be based on: (1) observations of each person's natural aptitude for certain tasks; (2) selection of people to suit tasks; and (3) training in the most effective use of the body. Efficiency is based on the most appropriate use of strength (how much to use); space (which direction in which to use it); time (how long to take in doing it); and the flow (whether it is free or restricted). States of rest and relaxation are distinguished. Discovering the appropriate period of rest is part of establishing the rhythm required for the task which lies at the basis for economy of human effort.

Chapter 2: The Appropriate Use of Movement

Observation and training will achieve the most economical

movement for a particular task. It is first necessary to decide whether the task needs a light or a strong approach and whether the action is fluent or in some way restricted (bound). Then the task is to determine the most appropriate path in space for each action – whether it is direct or indirect as well as the most effective time in which to achieve it (how quick or how slow). The eight basic combinations of weight (strength), space (direction) and time (duration) are identified in basic effort actions together with their symbols in notation. Some actions are capable of being executed by more than one approach and then it is most important to take into account the natural effort characteristics of the individual performing the task.

Chapter 3: Effort Training

When people are trained in the eight basic efforts, understanding should help the choice of appropriate actions. The approach is twofold: general effort training and specific. The aim of the first is towards bodily awareness in effort sequences, and of the second to discover and understand the practice of the rhythms contained in them. These can be carried out both with and without the actual tools involved. Good transitions from one effort to another are important, for it is only by carrying out the entire sequence required that real economy of effort occurs.

Chapter 4: Selection and Effort Balance

Overspecialization can be counter-productive and in selection for a job the whole effort make-up of the individual needs to be taken into account. No matter what the task, the individual undertaking it needs a balance. Merely being able to undertake a special action well is usually not enough. Each individual has to be able to balance the efforts required by being able to perform contrasting efforts to assist the adjustment and prevent fatigue. Building an all-roundedness in effort skill recognizes that while man may be working with machines, he is not a machine but a finely tuned human being.

Chapter 5: The Observation and Specification of Job-Efforts

The object in carrying out any task should be to perform it in the simplest and least strenuous manner. This means discovering both the simple shape of the movements required together with the appropriate rhythms to achieve the greatest economy: a time–space pattern for the task. Where necessary, the job can be broken down into its components and each stage practised before putting all together with the appropriate transitions. This is the basis from which to assess efficiency.

Chapter 6: Psychological Aspects of Effort Control

Man is not simply a physical being. Besides carrying out a task, man has also an attitude to it: he may struggle against it, or indulge in it. Each of the four 'motion factors' – time, weight, space and flow can be struggled against or indulged in, and the propensity of an individual towards one or other of these motion factors may be the predominant (though not the only) character trait. The awareness of the psychological aspects in effort control should help management and workforce more easily to appreciate each other since, no matter what the task or status (manual or clerical, employer or employee), effort qualities and working rhythms are involved. Attitudes can change and be changed through the skilful training and control of effort.

Chapter 7: Thinking in Terms of Effort.

We will not achieve adequate efficiency and economy until we learn to think in terms of the whole of the effort involved – time, weight, space and flow – instead of limiting conceptions to matters of age, sex and overtime. Acting on proper analysis outweighs practices built on prejudice and trial and error approaches. It is vital to discover the reasons for individual effort failure and to overcome these by effort training. Similarly, it is possible to improve group and team work, observe and act on body language in meetings and apply the findings to other aspects of community living, such as work in hospitals, throughout the arts and in schools. Thinking in terms of effort is one of the keys to discovering greater command of life and living.

The publication of *Effort* clearly marks the great shift of emphasis in Laban's work. He has left behind the dance and performance side of his investigation and activity. Proof of the value of his theory in all walks of life, he shows that the same principles are in operation no matter what the activity.

Again, there are many thought-provoking statements of a universal nature. For example, 'Rhythmic movement is pleasant, partly because its energy-saving qualities are felt by the operator and partly because it gives to the actions a certain perfection.' We long for specific examples but again find only the non-particular. 'Suppose a man has to push a heavy object away.' In vain we seek a name for the object and a context for the pushing. Taken overall, however, this book is more easy to read than most of Laban, probably due to the collaborative hand of Lawrence. Remarkable credit to Laban's own flexibility is the fact that, even at the age of seventy, he could adjust to the new calls on and openings for his understanding of movement.

So far, Lisa Ullmann had been looking for work for Laban and following him and his lead in whatever commissions came along. But the post-war reconstruction also gave her the chance to establish an area, built on Laban theory, which she could corner as her own. When the war finally came to an end, Lisa, a teacher, not a dancer, was able to build on work she had already pioneered in education.

Helped by the good auspices of Wigman-trained Diana Jordan, Lisa had already made an impact on the teaching world in Britain through Workers' Educational Association classes, short holiday courses and courses for institutions like Bedford College of PT. There was a definite responsiveness to the Laban approach to physical education and to development of the work first outlined in *Gymnastics and Dance*. Local education authorities, government inspectors and teachers were looking for greater guidance in facing a more creative approach to physical expression and fitness and needed a book providing understanding in the teaching of what had come in this country to be called Modern Dance, so Laban brought out a book entitled:

Modern Educational Dance

Published in 1948 by Macdonald and Evans, *Modern Educational Dance* reflects Lisa Ullmann's work, and her 'widespread activity in British schools and teacher training' are acknowledged as having made a contribution to the book. Laban refers to his own Czechoslovakian (not Hungarian) origin and says that his background study began in Paris where the form was '*la danse libre*', becoming later 'central European Dance'. Significantly, there is no mention of German dance or dance of German origin, nor of any of his work or publications in Germany between the wars.

Strangely enough, it was not Lisa Ullmann that Laban chose to test his ideas against, but a young woman, one of four first-year students who began training when Lisa opened her Manchester Art of Movement Studio in 1946. This was Veronica Tyndale-Biscoe, who had originally trained under Joan Goodrich at Bedford College but had not found that the work there had enough to do with the whole person to satisfy her. It was a visit by Laban and Lisa to Bedford that opened her awareness and renewed her interest in what she described as 'a complete revelation' – she felt she had found what she had been looking for.

While on the Studio course at Manchester, she was asked to visit a nursery school to observe the movement of very young children and even babies, to report back to Laban who was compiling material for his book. It was she who observed the laughing, crying baby, wriggling and expressing a good deal by counter-tension, arms and legs in action: a total experience.

Laban's understanding enabled him to give her observations full weight and to accept them as factual evidence for Chapter 1. He was pleased to have someone to act as a sounding-board and sought to involve Veronica in the writing of the book. At first, he gave her ideas to write up and she loyally struggled with them, but found it hard work since it all had to take place *after* 4.30 p.m. At the end of a long day in the Studio on the Oxford Road, physically trying to assimilate ideas, she would travel out to Laban in Didsbury to work mentally till nine or ten each evening, writing up the concepts.

After a while, Veronica explained to Laban that it was impossible for her to do both things well. She took a rest period from the evening writing, but not long after resumed trying to help him.

This time, her aim became to assist him with his English (which she described as 'impossible'), seeking to make his sentences 'easier to understand'.[9] She was willing and flattered but still found it hard to believe that a student just at the beginning of her career could act as a competent assistant to a theoretician rapidly approaching the end of his. Years later, in an interview, she was adamant that *Modern Educational Dance* was not her writing, that she found it turgid, dry and theoretical and only regarded her contribution as 'tiny'.

There are five chapters and an introduction in the 104-page book written 'in the conviction that, at an age when the child's natural urge to dance has sufficiently developed, it is possible, and of educational value, to base dance tuition upon the principles of contemporary movement research'.

Summary of Content

Introduction

The trends of social changes throughout the ages are echoed in the dances of each period, but, unlike the other arts, dance has scant records. There is a brief survey, with some pioneers and their innovations mentioned – notably Jean-Georges Noverre, in looking forward to a new movement expression, and Isadora Duncan, looking back to draw from the freedom of Ancient Greece. We should learn from earlier ages and attempt once more to unite all sides of man by exploring 'a rich movement life'. Dance movements can help to free the soul of man and counterbalance the tensions and restrictions of modern industrial life. Training in the new dance is underpinned by recognition of effort elements embodied in movement sequences. Its aims are to foster flow and strength in movement, to preserve spontaneity, and to inculcate creativity and artistic expression.

Chapter 1: Dancing through the Age Groups

By contrasting what is natural and fresh in the baby and young child with the more restricted, isolated and unbalanced movements which emerge as it grows older, Laban points out the need for an activity which will release the flow and cleanse the spirit. In educational dance, then, young children can achieve greater balance. They can be taught movement observation and encouraged to develop some basic analysis. Through imaginative stimuli, they learn confidence in the use of space and flow.

Chapter 2: Sixteen Basic Movement Themes

A two-way process is at work: mind influences movement; movement influences mind. Movement themes are used instead of standard exercises. Sixteen basic movement themes are described, but it is up to each teacher to use the ideas creatively to stimulate the students to move and dance, according to their aptitude and ability. The themes begin with basic awareness of body, the body in space, quality of action, time taken and the nature of the flow of movement.

Throughout the chapter the complexity grows, from the use of simple occupational rhythms to the discovery of the moods expressed in challenging combinations of efforts.

Chapter 3: Rudiments of a Free Dance Technique

Each of the eight effort actions is considered in turn, with the aim generally of giving the teacher some practical appreciation underlying rules of effort co-ordination. Again, the importance of these actions is stressed in the development of harmony and balance in each individual.

Chapter 4: The Conception of the Sphere of Movement

An abstract discussion of the body in space related to the centre, the surfaces and edges of a cube. First, the teacher is introduced to the sphere of space around the body and then, as a means of orientation in space, to the dimensions. This leads to consideration of 26 space directions, all radiating from the centre of the space, including the *space-diagonals* which are between the dimensions, the *diameters* between dimensions and diagonals, and the *diametrals* between two diagonals. This is followed by a discussion of ways in which flow, shape and rhythm combine in movement and dance sequences and styles.

Chapter 5: The Observation of Movement

The recommendation is to begin to observe human actions in terms of effort, since this way the observer remains objective. These in their turn can be broken down into the individual's use of space, time and weight, and observation of whether he indulges or fights these. Observation can then assist the teacher in appreciating certain traits of character, identifying conflicting effort habits and helping to substitute these for more harmonious combinations. Realizing that movement is the essence of life enables the teacher to become aware not just of the external manifestations but also of the mental state of the individual mover. The overall aim is for wholeness in the person and integration within the whole. Then the balanced character can seek a harmonious integration within the group and in the wider society.

We miss the Laban idealism and educational vision which he conveyed in *Children's Gymnastics and Dance*. This is unfortunately not the sort of writing to inspire youngsters or their teachers. An individual would have to be dedicated to struggle through the technical details, and teachers need to bring to it their lively imaginations to be able to translate it into engaging educational activity. Where is the 'engage them first; theory later' approach which Laban talked of in the earlier work? Reviewing a revised edition of *Modern Educational Dance* some sixteen years after its first publication, Veronica Sherborne could only regret the fact that the book in its present form did not 'contain the dynamic power and warmth of feeling which he (Laban) conveyed through movement'.[10] She was already aware that, pioneer work though the original was, the time was already ripe for a re-interpretation of Laban's discoveries in a way which might communicate something of his enthusiasm, insight and untiring search.

By the autumn of that year (1948), Lisa Ullmann had obtained Ministry of Education approval for a year's one-year emergency training course for teachers. More and more she was to focus on the Studio and the training of teachers. Laban took up the challenges of applying his work in other areas.

While still exploring with Lawrence the movement possibilities in industry, an invitation from Esme Church arrived for Laban to visit her newly founded Northern Theatre School at Bradford. Church had briefly watched Laban at work on a British Drama League Summer Course at York and knew immediately that she wanted him on the visiting staff of her school. Laban agreed but, as he was battling against illness, he took along with him one of the students from the Studio, Geraldine Stephenson.

Laban worked with the (mainly ex-service) students at the Theatre School, giving training in movement and directing a number of mime plays, taking the cross-Pennine trains several times a week when he was in good health. When in Manchester he was still working at the Studio as well as supervising the industrial side with F.C. Lawrence. In March of that year he had renewed acquaintance with Joan Littlewood and Theatre Workshop when they moved back to Manchester.

Mastery of Movement on the Stage

As a result of this and other work with actors, it seemed opportune for Laban to write his next book, *Mastery of Movement on the Stage*. In the preface, Laban acknowledges former pupils and co-workers, explaining that the text is a digest of many of his lectures and talks shared with them. Geraldine Stephenson recalls some of the many conversations she and Laban had crossing the Pennines. Valerie Preston-Dunlop certainly assisted Laban in assimilating the material and recalls being surprised to find that the moves Laban uses in Chapter 1 were those that Knust had published earlier for his dance notation students.

The book is 190 pages in length and contains a prologue and three chapters, each of which is divided into two parts.

Summary of Content

Prologue

A great deal is touched upon in this introduction. It begins clearly by explaining that movement is carried out with a purpose – whether that purpose is conscious or subconscious. Any actions we undertake can be expressed in a wide variety of ways, as the example of Eve in the Garden of Eden, taking the apple, can amply illustrate. Movement both expresses and communicates many things.

The further into the text we travel, the more the focus jumps. We are told that several different factors affect movement, including character, state of mind, environment, locality, atmosphere and epoch. Actors need to make effective entrances and exits and need to understand the nature of individual and other relationships communicated through the grouping.

Voice is another aspect of movement and when words are part of the scene, physical gestures will tend to be less elaborate, though just as important in their communication. Laban dips into dramatic theory as well as movement theory, contrasts pure dancing with dance-drama and in diagrammatic form draws attention to the fact that movement is central to each of the living arts as well as work and worship. Above all, human movement is 'the common denominator of the dynamic art of the theatre'.

Chapter 1: Part I – Movement and the Body

This takes us once more into the abstract with another look at our old friends space, weight, time and flow as well as another look at 'fighting against' and 'indulging in' these factors. The reader is left to 'invent scenes' for practice. Laban then sets up a basis for 'The Analysis of Bodily Actions' and gives us 81 of Knust's moves.

Part II outlines 'Variations of Elementary Movements' taking the number of moves to 306. All extremely technical and abstract in their presentation – enough to make the average actor give up the struggle very early. Should anyone ever get to Move 306, they are presented with some advice: study these and variations of them 'in connection with short dance or mime scenes'. Where, one wonders, is the holistic approach so frequently recommended by Rudolf Laban?

Chapter 2: Part I – The Significance of Movement

A brief introduction to the language of rhythm before we move to a discussion of movement which flows from the centre of the body and movement which flows the other way – from the periphery of the space surrounding the body towards the centre. Several of the themes mentioned earlier are picked up here: efforts, rhythm, style, the nature of the theatre and the difference between drama and ballet. Laban claims that movement is more significant than words and so in his view mime becomes greater than drama. The discussion is rounded off with a few (welcome) examples and things are further illuminated by his suggestions for vocal expressions which can result from, for instance, saying the simple word 'No', using the effort qualities in the inflection.

Chapter 2: Part II – The Roots of Mime

This section is again largely theoretical. He is greatly concerned with mime and theatre as purveyors of values and the struggles which arise from them. There are some examples followed through with a little detail, mostly in relation to archetypal characterizations and morality type virtues. Effort actions are looked at in some detail and related to characterization. Inner attitudes and shadow actions are also touched upon.

Chapter 3: Part I – The Study of Movement Expression

The best way to develop good expressive movement for the stage, Laban declares, is to practise performing scenes – suggestions for scenes and mimes are given. But first Laban considers various approaches to rhythm. Space, weight and time can each dominate rhythmic patterns at certain times. He then goes into a more detailed outline of Greek metric form which he relates to certain moods of expression. The section concludes with scenes and situations for development, some group scenes and some symbolic scenes.

Chapter 3: Part II – Three Mime Plays

These are each outlined in a different format and commented upon from different standpoints.

This is Laban's longest work in English but because, for Laban, all the world is *the stage*, he tries to cover too much ground and as a result does not travel with us to any discernible destination. It is a difficult work to read if it is approached in the usual way of reading a text, expecting logical, step-by-step progression. Like so much of his other writing, it is less frustrating if read as a series of thought-rounds and in the knowledge that Laban is not the kind of teacher who is interested in developing an argument in a linear approach but a theoretician who works by presenting related patterns. Otherwise it is too easy to miss the stimulation that the book can afford.

Even the title is misleading, for one might be forgiven for believing that within these covers lies the secret of 'how to achieve mastery of movement on the stage'. The only section with logical development is that covering the dance exercises from Knust – a section which stands out as not being in harmony with the rest of the work. The simple scenes and scenarios (which anyway seem more Laban) are more appropriate and helpful for actors. For the initiated, there is plenty of food for thought, whether it comes in the form of provocative generalization or as a statement of the obvious.

Many of these sentences could be developed into a chapter, a book or a series of practical sessions. Many an experienced movement teacher could develop a term's classes out of statements such as: 'When two or more players are to meet on the stage, they have to make their entrance, approach one another (either touching or keeping a due distance) and later they have to separate and make their exit.' But the actor needs the 'given circumstances' – a basic story line.

Or the experienced ballet teacher could find challenging teaching material in statements like: 'Movements performed in ballet have lost their connection with the primitive drives of man.' Or anyone might ponder over statements like: 'Modern industrial worker's actions are very often confined to one or other of the fundamental rhythms determined by the ancient Greeks.'

In the general text, such declarations are offputting if we expect general introduction followed by progressive exercises. Taken as paragraphs for pondering, (or as text to stimulate one's own practical sessions), however, it is a book which can be seen to be in the Laban tradition of evoking rather than evolving, stimulating rather than prescribing.

Movement Psychology

Movement Psychology is an unfinished, unpublished collaborative manuscript of 77 pages, handwritten by William Carpenter. Carpenter appears to have become a patient at the Withymead Centre for Psychotherapy shortly after his marriage broke up and remained assisting the work at that Centre, which is where he first met Laban. It seems that the two got on so well that Laban invited him to Addlestone, where he lived in a caravan on the grounds, seeing Laban and working together with him on the book on a regular basis. This collaboration continued from 1952 until William Carpenter died in 1954. Laban's confidence in his own grasp of psychology seemed insufficient to sustain his drive to continue with the work alone.

For once, however, Laban was attempting a work stimulated by current ideas and a growing interest in applying his theory to 'inner states', some related to psychology, (especially that understanding of the human psyche as propounded by Carl Gustav Jung), others explored as a result of Laban's own intuitive understanding.

True to his more abstract concern of his period in the UK, Laban chose to begin to codify and relate his effort theory to inner traits of personality – or, as he puts it, the interaction between inner states of mind and outer actions. The manuscript is at the stage of exploring terms and terminology, attempting to build a language related to recognized personality types, yet extended by Laban's own observations on effort and movement theory. As it has survived, the manuscript consists mainly of charts and diagrams associating 'Inner Attitudes with Externalized Drives'. At times, we are again aware of Laban's lack of mastery of English as he uses archaic words like 'irrelated' and 'adream', inadequately discussed terms like 'passion' and 'spell' and awkward phrases such as 'yield with' and 'contend against'.

Summary of Content

Movement Psychology begins with some useful definitions establishing the field of exploration. The work is structured around Laban's ideas on *effort* – which now becomes 'the sequence of inner attitudes and external drives which activate an action' – while *action* is seen as 'a bodily movement expressed through the *motion factors* of weight, space, time and flow performed for a functional purpose with a measure of conscious volition'.

Motion factors are then related to the four *mental factors* identified by Jung (though no mention of Jung is made). Sensing (sensory perception through the five senses) is revealed in the quality, weight or pressure (light or strong) of movement. Thinking (formation of ideas through intellectual reflective reasonings) is revealed in movement through the use of space and the capacity to focus (direct or indirect). Intuiting (insight by the mind without reasoning) is seen in movement as time changes (quicker or slower). Lastly, feeling (the emotion of liking or disliking) is revealed in our movements in changes of flow (freer or more bound). Each motion factor has subdivisions into *elements* – here polarized into:

Weight – light and strong
Space – flexible and direct
Time – sustained and quick
Flow – free and bound.

These elements can be seen either to yield (which Laban calls the feminine element) or contend (which Laban calls the masculine element) in relation to the related motion factor.

Laban lists the eight efforts which he now calls 'the eight basic working actions' and provides four further divisions or classifications – referred to as *inner participations* – concerned with the individual's approaches to these actions:

1. Where 'attending' (the mind turned, waiting for action) is the stressed component (seen in the use of space)
2. Where 'intending' (the mind motivated, poised to take action) is the stressed component (seen in use of weight)
3. Where 'deciding' (past and future meet in present commitment to take action) is the stressed component (seen in use of time)

4. Where 'adapting' (extrovert adjustment of self to the outer world and introverted adjustment of the conscious self to the subconscious) is the stressed component (seen in use of flow).

These are shown diagramatically in relation to the Effort Cube.

Sometimes the interplay between the components is cancelled out in what Laban calls *negatives*:

- *Intending* has the negative which he terms '*heavy*' and defines as 'the negatively neutral and impotent quality of *weight* in which the interplay of light and strong is cancelled by inertia which negates the receiving and transmitting intentions of sensing'.
- *Attending* has the negative which he calls '*adrift*' and defines as 'the negatively neutral quality of *space* in which the interplay of flexible and direct is cancelled by a disorientation which negates the reflective and attending aspects of thinking'.
- *Deciding* has the negative which he calls '*indecisive*' and defines as 'the negatively mental and dream quality of *time* in which the interplay of sustained and quick is cancelled by a timelessness which negates the relating of past and present and future in the decisions of intuiting'.
- *Adapting* has the negative which he calls '*irrelated*' (unrelated) and defines as 'the negatively neutral and frozen quality of *flow* in which the interplay of free and bound is cancelled by an emotional fixity which negates the extrovert or introverted aspects of the adapting and relating of feeling'.

Inner Quests

As individuals or in a role we adopt, we have what Laban calls *inner quests*. There are both inner and outer *wants*: as the character, what is my (overall) intending want?

1. What do I want in life?
2. What do I want in the play?
3. What do I want in the scene?
4. To whom or to what?

As well as these wants, there are inner and outer obstacles or resistances:

5. How (do I face it)? What means do I use?
6. When (do I face it)?
7. Where?
8. Why?
9. Who am I?
      What I am (inner)
      What I want to appear (outer).

Laban follows this by setting out tables detailing six sub/unconscious states which he lists as the *inner attitudes*. These are normally initiated in the unconscious mind but because of the two-way process, can be activated by bodily movements. Each attitude is revealed in our movements as a compound of two elements. They are identified in three pairs of opposites:

STABLE   MOBILE
NEAR   REMOTE
AWAKE   DREAMING

Each of these *inner attitudes* is classified in a detailed table setting out the motion factors, the mental factors, the inner participations and the inner quests. Unconscious effort motifs are related to shadow moves and each interpreted in terms of personality traits. Finally each is diagrammatically outlined in relation to the effort cube and a flow chart.

These are followed by classifications of the *externalized drives* – the four mental states which are 'motivated by the subconscious inner attitudes and which activate us into the conscious actions. Each drive is revealed as a compound of three elements of movement.' Externalized drives are identified as:

- Doing – (exerting–reacting) which is flowless and associated with stable, near, awake.
- Passion – (constructing–destroying) which is spaceless, and associated with mobile, near, dreaming.
- Spell – (dominating–surrounding) which is timeless, and associated with stable, remote, dreaming.

- Vision – (ideas–problems) which is weightless and associated with mobile, remote, awake.

Further flow diagrams present a visual representation of what he calls the 'Confluence of Externalized Drives'.

It is an interesting manuscript, ultimately frustrating to work through since so much new terminology is left without adequate commentary, detailed example or explanation.

Ever since his early days in Munich (around 1910), Laban had occupied himself with developing a notation system which would enable dances, like music, to be written down. Through the years, he and his students wrestled with the staff on which to write and the symbols by which best to record movement. In 1927 as we have seen this system was officially given to the dance world. In subsequent years, several Notation Conferences were held and many refinements and other changes took place. The ideas spread. Notation Bureaux were set up in Hamburg, in Berlin and, in 1940, in New York. Major dance works on both sides of the Atlantic were being written down and Labanotation was being taught in many dance schools and universities. By the early 1950s it was evident that Laban needed to re-establish his authority in this rapidly developing field. It was long overdue for Laban to record his principles in English and establish clearly the copyright.

Principles of Dance and Movement Notation

Summary of Content

In the *Preface*, Laban acknowledges that his notation is built on the same principles as those on which the choreography of Beauchamp and Feuillet was established 300 years earlier. He mentions four: the central line separating movements on the left from those of the right; dividing this middle line by bar lines denoting the metrical division of time; directional signs and shape symbols guiding the person moving in space; and using special emphasis signs to indicate basic bodily actions.

Laban pays tribute to Dussia Bereska's 'inspiring advice' and 'deciding influence' on the rhythmic partitioning of Feuillet's metrical bar-line intervals. It was she who suggested the symbols could be written in different lengths to indicate the relative duration of the movement. He also acknowledges that it was Jooss whose idea it was to extend the notation to include the upper parts of the body in separate columns. He expresses his indebtedness to Valerie Preston-Dunlop for arranging the examples, which he recalls as something of a dogsbody task, but her logical mind and understanding of notation clearly helps the later sections.

The first part of this 56-page booklet, 'Movement Notation and the Fields of its Application', is devoted to the background to notation and the justification for it. Laban sets the record straight – he began his quest for a script 25 years before the publication of his system in 1928. He had grappled with the idea of a dance notation since his days in Paris and worked most purposefully at it during the 1920s. He also establishes his credentials by mentioning famous choreographers and musicians who have encouraged him.

He makes clear to whom the copyright belongs when he declares quite plainly, 'I discovered the principles and invented the basic symbols.' He says that his fundamental signs remain unaltered, though later pioneers and practitioners have added knowledge and experience. It is this notation that has enabled dance to be recorded and so establish a dance literature. The Second World War left Albrecht Knust in Germany notating dances, saw Sigurd Leeder in London developing the script and Ann Hutchinson in New York spreading its use in recording professional dances.

The Second Part, 'Introducing the necessity for thinking in terms of movement and the explanations of the graphs', explains that by depicting movements through a series of graphic symbols the reader gains more than a description in words could offer. In order to read the notation adequately it is important to think in terms of movement. Then, as a lead into the text of the second part, consisting mainly of graphs of movement motifs with only incidental verbal descriptions of some fundamental movement ideas and their symbols, he outlines the general principles underlying any kind of movement notation. It is perhaps ironic that this booklet which appeared just two years before he died should be the last of all his ten major publications. Other areas of his influence were those where the demand was most immediate and Laban, in spite of the difficulties, attempted to provide points of reference in writing.

Various articles appeared in the *Laban Art of Movement Guild Magazine* between this last booklet and Laban's death in July, 1958. A number of severe illnesses suggested that Laban might not live long and those around were anxious to record in print as many of his ideas as possible, so items on general topics, specific topics and anecdotal recall appeared in the magazine under his name right up to and beyond his death.

Movement notation remains the area of his pioneering for which Laban is most universally acknowledged. The rest of his work, as he himself anticipated, needs some translating and interpreting to make it accessible and useful.

Part Four
CLARIFYING LABAN'S BASIC IDEAS

'. . . he was a genius.'

Sir Robert Stephens, actor.

Clarifying Laban's Basic Ideas

Now the task is to take all this activity and outside influence on Laban and, placing it alongside his experience and writing, attempt to gain a comprehensive view of his theory and practice. We are seeking to establish a clear foundation from which we might make full use of his concepts. The quest is to establish what might be seen as basic and esssential Laban.

In attempting such a codification, we should remind ourselves of two caveats in Laban's wisdom: The first is to *avoid formula*. Life is movement, flux, change, and has many exceptions and contradictions. But this should not prevent us from trying to *formulate* the main precepts and principles he discovered. The second is *not to expect a method*, which he pointed out would only lead to a rigidity of approach. Nevertheless this should not deflect us from trying at least to be *methodical*.

How, then, should we attempt such a task? We know that Laban thinks not in words but 'in terms of movement'. 'Movement thinking', he explains in *Mastery of Movement*, 'could be considered as a gathering of impressions of the happenings in one's own mind . . .'. Laban was constantly looking for relationships in these impressions, for patterns, or for what he called the 'hidden order' – to help to make sense of it all.

Identifying Patterns

It would seem prudent to select the essentials of Laban's findings and present them in his way: that is, by recognizing not a scientific theory but *patterns of discovery*. Then, having identified the patterns, order them to give greater insight, and provide understanding which can the more easily be put to practical use.

The logic followed here is first to look at Laban's underlying beliefs, what we have called *the universal pattern* in which all movement takes place. Then we focus on the *human pattern*, identifying initially what Laban requires of us as basic to the study of movement. This leads into the patterns relating to the *nature of movement, the instrument of movement* and so into the *main principles of movement*. Finally, as if to come full circle, we focus on those patterns which *link man's movement to the universal*.

This rationale has led to the identification of 32 principles or patterns which seem to convey the basic elements of Laban's movement ideas. Some are based on more tangible, factual discoveries, while others outline his more generalized views of the world. Together, they show Laban's positive outlook together with his sense of the wholeness and the unity of experience.

10 The Universal Pattern – Underlying Beliefs

Pattern 1: All the World's in Motion

'The whole visible universe is Motion', Laban declared in an article published posthumously in *LAMG Magazine* in 1959.[1] His prime focus was on the human individual and his/her movement, but he saw the movement of man not in isolation but as part of an entire cosmos of movement. Everything, everywhere, he pointed out, is on the move. In the heavens, the clouds, the stars in the Milky Way, the sun, the moon and the planets are all changing and travelling. Planet earth is a part of this pattern. The waves roll in the seas, the tides are ebbing and flowing. On the earth and beneath it, there are rumblings, quakes and slides. Fire and flame rise up, consume and are consumed. Movement exists in the very composition of matter too: in the mineral, in the crystal and in every microscopic unit of each organism.

The rare thing about the earth is that it contains living movement. Here on earth, 'there exist several milliards of living beings . . . such as plants, microbes, insects, fishes and all the higher animals . . .'. Though plants are fixed in the soil, there is movement in their growth, flowering and production of seeds.

Pattern 2: Related and Recurring Movement Patterns

'In the forests covering great districts of the globe,' Laban continues, 'in the miraculous gardens at the bottom of the sea and in the midst of fantastic clouds in the air, we are amazed to see all kinds of animals carrying on their work and on certain occasions obeying some mysterious compulsion to perform seemingly purposeless movements'.

Patterns occur and re-occur. In all this activity there are movements such as bodies revolving round a body at the centre; recurring shapes and structures, amongst which is the notion of the cellular structure of matter.

> Atoms of living matter, constituting the cells, do not differ essentially from the atoms of inanimate matter. The only difference is that in living compounds, the atoms of one element, carbon, play a prominent role. The atoms build up elements which compound into various groupings constituting the different kinds of matter. Atoms consist of different numbers of little sparks, called electrons which circulate around a central spark like planets round the sun.[2]

Laban's experience led him to distinguish between movement governed by external forces and movement generated from within. His quest for a sense of unity, of structure, of purpose, encouraged him to feel that there could be a relationship between the two and that greater understanding of this relationship could lead to a better quality of life. Man needs to understand his nature and its links with Nature. Then, by working with Nature, he can gain greater insight into his own nature.

Pattern 3: Quality of Life seen in Movement

It is the degree of sophistication of movement that helps Laban identify the quality of life. This enables him to point out that though plants, animals and humans can all move, motivated, as it were, from within, plant movement is limited to growth and reproduction while animals have greater freedom of movement, are more flexible, have greater range and employ it for more complex purposes. Animals are able to move in ways which at first sight seem less purposeful (in play, for instance) as well as to satisfy the needs of survival and response to others of their species.

Amidst all this activity is man and in man is all manner of activity. The range of human movement is the greatest of all and the most complex.

Pattern 4: Movement the Common Experience

'Looking at the whole innate and acquired impulses of man, one is tempted to search for a common denominator.'[3] And Laban declares confidently that 'this denominator . . . is movement with all its spiritual implications.'

> Man likes to think that he has a role which is the penetrator of all kinds of mysteries through the activities of his mind. The mystery of his own doings awakens his curiosity earlier and more strongly than most other riddles of the universe.

When one takes all this into account, and begins to see not just that all things move but notices how and where and why they move, it is hard not to draw the conclusion that there is one single factor which runs through everything – it is not just that everything moves but, especially when we examine living matter, we see that there is nothing we can distinguish as life unless it reveals movement.

Pattern 5: Movement the Unifying Experience

Laban's observations lead him to the belief that 'Movement is the unifying factor of all existence'.[4] Once it has been seen that movement runs through every aspect of living reality, it is not a great step to realize that movement brings together and binds experience making it one.

It is the mystery of man's movement which awakened Laban's interest and though it remains by far the most difficult to understand, he finds himself with a special mission – to try to make sense of it all in an attempt to gain greater insight into the riddle of existence.

Pattern 6: Movement the Basic Experience

Everything that we discover about life, we discover through movement. Light waves reach the eye, sound waves contact the ear. Both smell and taste involve movement. Above all, our capacity to touch and move to gain further experience confirms our awareness. Existence is movement. Movement is a confirmation and an affirmation of life. When we move, we are part of the living universe.

1. Rudolf Laban as an art student in Paris, 1900.

2. Drawing by Laban showing spatial tension between three figures, ?1915–16.

3 & 4. Drawings by Laban illustrating 'Dance exercises in space'.

3

4

5. Drawing by Laban, ?1911–12. This sketch is typical of those Laban produced for commercial use while in Munich.

6. A similar grouping humorously recreated in a dance class at Monte Verità, Ascona, in 1913. The dancer on the right is Laban's first wife, Maja Lederer von Laban.

7 & 8. Examples of Kinetographie Laban, undated. Figure 8 shows
Kurt Jooss.

9–11. Diagrams and figures used in 'The Development of Laban's Dance Script', *Schrifttanz* No. 2, October 1928, from a lecture given by Laban to the German Dance Congress in Essen, 1928.

9

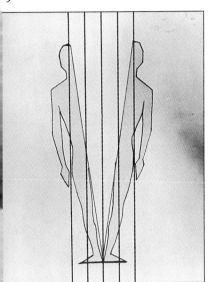

10

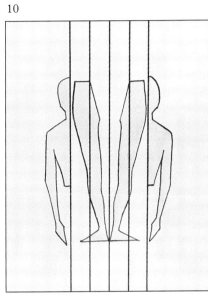

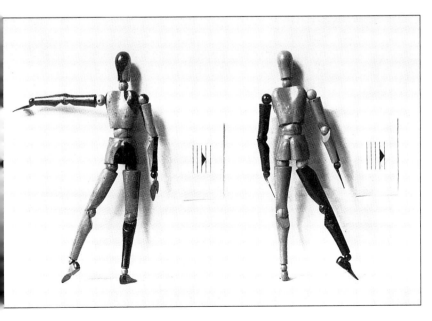

11

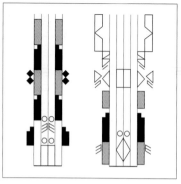

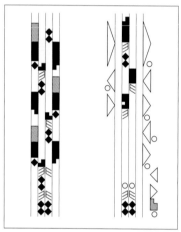

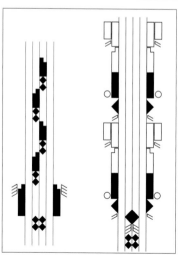

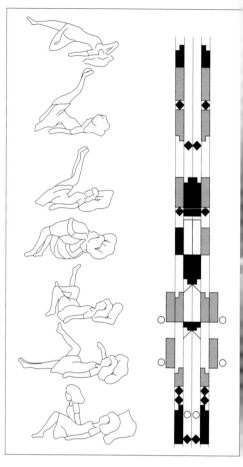

12. An early form (1930) of Kinetographie Laban, here applied to movement therapy. The first three diagrams (*left*) show crawling exercises for curvature of the spine; the fourth (*above*) show the use of Laban's system to record hysterical convulsions. (The original notation is by Suzanne Ivers; these diagrams have been redrawn for clarity.)

13. Scene 1,
'The Gentlemen
in Black',
The Green Table
by Kurt Jooss,
with notation.

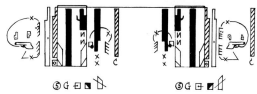

14. Notation for a tango.

15. Press photograph of Laban at his fiftieth birthday celebrations, displaying symbols from his recently published notation system.

16. Laban and Kurt Jooss at Dartington Hall in 1939, looking at the score for *The Green Table*.

Basics for Understanding Movement

The way to learn more about this common denominator is through movement itself, actively exploring with the body. But there are also four interrelated, crucial functions of the mind required for fuller understanding:

Pattern 7: Tools for Discovery of Movement

Movement Observation

Laban had a natural propensity towards observation of movement; most likely, as has been suggested, due in part to growing up with a lively body and mind and being often left on his own during his early days. This was helped by the fact that he also had the good fortune to travel a great deal to strange lands where he encountered many amazing sights and experiences.

Learning to see and notice movement from broad impression down to the finest detail is the important beginning to any greater understanding. Making mental and written notes will help the process and start the awareness of its fundamental nature.

Movement Analysis

Once we become accustomed to noticing movement, we start to ask what is moving? where is it moving? and how is it moving? A breakdown of which limbs are in action begins. This subdivision of aspects of the movement feeds back into making the observation keener and builds general awareness and appreciation. Further Laban patterns help with this analysis.

Movement Memory

Most people can recall scenes and incidents, sounds, voices and tones, but few find it easy at first to remember movements. Keener observation and analysis are the key to improving movement memory. It is important to develop this side of the mind in developing the capacity to understand the meaning of movement.

Movement Imagination

The key to good movement imagination arises from the development of keen observation during movement experience. Once movement images begin to come naturally to the mind, various other associations can be made and an altogether more resourceful use of movement starts. One image becomes linked with another, stimulating subsequent ideas in an altogether creative process.

Pattern 8: Thinking in Terms of Movement

All this leads to the senses responding more actively to all kinds of movement taking place around. Laban stresses the importance of seeing work and recreation, doing and dancing, in terms of movement. It is not enough simply to observe the activity, but more essential to focus in on the movement which goes to make that activity. It is rather a case of making sure that we see the wood when we look at the trees. Once we start 'thinking in terms of movement', we can observe the patterns and comprehend its nature and consequences more clearly.

Pattern 9: The Power and Potential of Movement

One of the first things that impressed Laban in his observation of movement was the power and significance of its impact. He witnessed the war dances of some groups where he noticed the participants could build up a state of aggression before facing combat, and the Dervishes, whose wild whirling brought them into a state of religious ecstasy. In this hypnotic condition they seemed able to resist pain and their muscle tissues showed no after-effect from needles and nails which pierced the skin. Movement, he realized, could have surprising effects on blood flow and circulation.

Pattern 10: The Two-way Process of Movement

Laban held that movement both affects and is affected by inner states. Movement arises from an inner impulse and in its turn the movements will affect the inner impulse and the general state of being. How we move affects and reflects both moods and feelings. Standing upright with arms open to the sides gives a very different feeling from being crouched and huddled up. When we feel confident we move differently from when we are depressed and downcast. It is possible to change a mood by moving in a certain way and, conversely, mood will change the movement pattern.

The body is not only an instrument of expression but also an instrument of impression: there is a two-way traffic of sending and receiving. Movement affects the body, mind and spirit; mind and spirit affect the body and its movement. Life is not all ecstasy or combat, but the same principles are at work wherever we move.

hand shake experience

Pattern 11: Imitation

A strong influence in movement habits is the phenomenon of following or picking up the movement patterns of others. This is especially influential in role models where, in an attempt to be like someone else, we take over certain movement patterns.

Imitation is a strong element in the way we learn to stand, walk, sit and so on in childhood and in the ways in which we associate ourselves with desirable groups. It is also an important primitive factor in learning to cope with, understand or even come to grips with others intuitively by assuming their movement patterns. It embodies something of that 'magical' power of movement.

Pattern 12: Adaptation – Factors Modifying Movement

Movement does not exist in isolation. We constantly adjust to and modify our movement to a number of different factors.

Movement may be:

i) externally motivated/modified
ii) internally motivated/modified.

It may be seen in, or as an interaction of:

i) the physical
ii) the psychological
iii) the metabolic
iv) the emotional.

Movement may be affected by such factors as:

- Epoch – the times in which we live (e.g. 19th, 20th or 21st century)
- Locality – where we are (e.g. palace or pub)
- Clothing – what we wear (e.g. its material, cut, relationship to body, style)

- Status – who we are (or who we think we are in relation to the rest of society)
- Age – how old we are or feel we are
  State of mind – how we feel generally (e.g. elated or depressed, clear or befuddled)
- Personality – what kind of a person we are (e.g. outgoing or indrawn)
- Atmosphere – the mood around (e.g. hostile or friendly)
- Environment – the physical conditions around (e.g. cold or warm)
- Situation – the overall circumstances (e.g. mealtime or accident).

Pattern 13: Function of Movement

'Man moves in order to satisfy a need,'[5] says Laban and in doing so he identifies two broad areas: the tangible (where one has an immediately, recognizable goal) and the intangible (where the goal is not so obviously seen). The needs can range from the very simple to the highly complex. Man moves:

- to do – a practical and clear purpose
- to understand – through thought or experience
- to express – giving form to feeling
- to dance – expressing the inexpressible.

Movement may involve no more than picking up something, or a simple change of position, or travelling from A to B. Or the need may involve acquiring greater skill in playing a game, making a meal, overcoming some aspect of the environment or improving dexterity at an occupational task. It may be a release of energy (as in shouting or jumping for joy) or a sublimation of it into more sustained and creative enterprises.

The possibilities are endless when we consider that we move for work, for living, in creating, in recreation and rehabilitation as well as in worship and all manner of personal and interpersonal situations.

Pattern 14: Levels of Response – Shadow Movements

We move both voluntarily and involuntarily. We react through movements of which we are conscious but we are also making movements unconsciously. Many people have unconscious mannerisms by which we easily recognize them, but all of us are also making postural and gestural movements of which we are quite unaware – and all these Laban called 'shadow' movements – movements performed without conscious volition yet expressing inner attitudes or externalized drives.

Shadow movements are, to the shrewd observer, equally revealing of character and personality, as well as possible limitations and capacities.

Pattern 15: Through the Body's Movement We Make Sense of the World

Since the living body is movement, knowing how it works and why is a basic means of understanding: through the body we experience size, time and texture. By analysing the purposes, processes and levels conveyed through movement, we have a means of greater comprehension of both what is within and around us. Through movement, we can come to terms with ourselves, as well as gaining insight into the nature of our being, our condition, relationships with others and our place in the universe.

Pattern 16: The Body and its Basic Movement

The Body: The Instrument of Movement

In its vertical and horizontal skeletal structure, Laban saw that the body maintained something of the stability of architecture. The three-dimensionality of pillars and arches is especially reflected in formal gesture. He observed the body's symmetrical structure with head and trunk placed centrally. Generally, where we have a single organ (like the nose, mouth, genitals), this is placed centrally while those of which we have two are symmetrically placed at each side of the body. The balanced body stands poised, striving outwards from the centre.

Like both Delsarte and Dalcroze, instrumentally Laban saw the body in three areas:

i) *the head* – containing all the senses (touch alone is possible elsewhere) and mental activity; the area of psychological activity.

ii) *the trunk* – where digestive, reproductive, purification and such like activity takes place; the area of metabolic activity.

iii) *the limbs* (arms and legs) – which are mainly concerned with activity related to mobility and gesture; the area of physical activity studied from the point of view of its function. Besides locomotion, legs help keep the balance, transfer the weight, leap, twist, turn the body. Gestures with arms and hands indicate, sweep, slice, penetrate and so on. Hands and fingers manipulate, hold, release, touch and the like.

Laban especially emphasizes the importance (for everyone as well as the performing artist) of the flexibility of the spine, the strength of the abdomen and the rhythm and expansion of the chest and lungs.

Breath and Breathing

Laban was very aware of the value of good breathing. Drawing breath is essential to life and though we all believe that it happens naturally, few really understand the process. The rhythm of chest and lower rib expansion which allows the intake of breath, he points out, is followed by the contraction of chest muscles which discharges the used air through mouth and nose. Breathing oxygenates the blood. It has a significant effect on well-being, the physical, emotional and intellectual potential of man. It is one of the prime means of developing the power to experience things to the full.

Flexibility and the Spinal Column

Laban points out the need for a renewed awareness of both straightness and suppleness in the spinal column. A good deal of man's natural poise has been lost through various influences of industrialization. Keeping the head up, eyes forward and shoulders down, and using only the necessary effort, enables good bodily alignment. The spine needs constantly to be lengthened against the gravitational pull.

The alignment of the spinal column in relation to the rest of the body is crucial because of its position and function in balancing the body and helping to maintain its upright stature. But there is also another important factor. Few people, Laban maintains, make full use of the turning, twisting power in the spine's complete mobility because they have either allowed their cartilage to stiffen or let their muscles become slack, losing much of the elasticity which Nature intended. Posture is part of expression as well as mobility.

Posture and Gesture

It is possible to gain understanding, Laban maintained, with the limbs and the trunk, just as with the brain. For both posture and gesture it is necessary to have a strengthened front abdominal wall, strong, tightened buttocks, upright spine. This is the best way for the body to stand against the gravitational pull and yet be responsive to action and interaction. Laban points out that, from its centre of gravity, the body is tensed in four directions, each leading towards a corner of the tetrahedron.

The Basic Principles of Movement – Towards a Vocabulary

So much for the body as the instrument of movement; now let's begin a process of analysis for better identification of the elements of movement itself. Laban first helps us recognize:

- where movement takes place
- how it takes place
- what its limitations are
- why it takes place.

In doing so, he recognized four motion factors: space, time, dynamic (weight) and flow, into which all movements can be analysed. Each motion factor has two 'elements' depending on whether the movement is seen to yield to or contend with the factor.

Pattern 17: The Body in Space

Where

The body moves in space. Movement is its visible aspect. Movement is change, and 'space,' Laban says, 'must be seen as the locality in which changes take place.'[6]

Means of Orientation

Laban calls the three-dimensional, globe-shaped space in which the body can operate (extending from the centre to the extension of the limbs) the *Kinesphere*. The term distinguishes the space an individual can use around the body from the more general space outside this. Within the Kinesphere, the body can take up a little space or extend to reach the perimeter.

The changes form a range of shapes as they alter from one state to another and Laban noted the factors involved in forming the shapes:

- *Dimension* – the three dimensions of height, width and depth enable Laban to identify movement which is predominantly in:

  i) an upwards–downwards direction
  ii) a sideways, right–left direction
  iii) a forwards–backwards direction.

- *Proximity* – where it takes place in relation to the body: close to it or away from it.
- *Planes* – relating to the dimensions, three planes are identified:

  i) related to action of the body when seen as if flat against a wall or standing within a frame: the 'door plane'
  ii) as if a flat surface stretched horizontally around the centre of the body: the 'table plane'
  iii) as if a flat surface stretched vertically from front to back: the 'wheel plane'.

- *Central/Peripheral Direction* – relationship to the centre: moving towards the body or away from it. A movement starting away from the body and moving towards it is said to be peripheral, while a movement which travels outwards is said to be central.
- *Elements of Space: Direct/Indirect* – whether taking the shortest route and so moving in a straight line (direct) or taking a more flexible, roundabout approach (indirect).

Pattern 18: The Body and its Movement Flow

All movement has a progression in which can be identified a degree or otherwise of fluidity. Some people let their movements travel easily, others hold back. The continuity of the movement can be subdivided for the purposes of analysis.

Elements of Flow – Free/Bound

Movement can at one extreme have a continuous smooth action in which case it is said to be 'free' flowing; at the other extreme the movement is held, stopped, limited, restricted and this time the flow is said to be 'bound'. Movements which flow freely often take time before they are stopped whereas those who easily curtail their movements often find fluency the problem. Between the two extremes there are, of course, all kinds of gradations from the totally free to the totally bound.

Pattern 19: The Body and its Movement Dynamic

One of the most important aspects of Laban's awareness of movement is his recognition that movement has a quality. We do not just move in space and time but with a degree of strength or weakness or intensity.

Elements of Weight – Strong/Weak (Light/Heavy)

Movements can be recognized as being heavier or lighter depending on the amount of energy and drive put into them. This makes a contribution to our appreciation of the function and value of movement. The energy of any movement is as much internal as external so consideration of dynamic is concerned also with the inner drive with which a movement is invested.

Pattern 20: The Body and its Rate of Moving

As well as existing in space, movement also exists in time. Any gesture may be undertaken at a different rate or duration giving an impression of speed or slowness.

Elements of Time – Quick/Slow (Accelerating/Decelerating)

The variety of use of time ranges from the extremely slow to the extremely fast. Movement may involve time freely and continuously or it may use an amount of time pattern or rhythm. Rest or pause may be seen as the inner gesture between two outer gestures.

Pattern 21: Tension

Tension is 'a drawing together, an alertness of all the senses, a tuning in to what is around, making a link, a connection within and without,'[7] says Laban. It can be seen as analogous to the striking of a chord in music.

Looked at negatively, it can be seen as the result of the fight against the gravitational pull; positively, it is the harnessing of inner and outer strengths. The force of tension is at the core of expression: intellectual, emotional and physical. We need tension to build strength and muscle in all these areas.

Tension is necessary but it has to be the appropriate amount of tension for the task or occasion; we need to avoid rigidity on the one hand or slackness on the other; the path we need to seek is that between laxity and hypertension.

Pattern 22: Human Effort

> In contemporary movement study, the active exercise of any power or faculty, whether physical or mental, is called effort. This active power, however, need not be extremely vigorous or laborious . . . an effort can take a calm or almost strainless form . . . especially when performed with acceptance or enjoyment.

Laban identifies contrasts in inner attitudes resulting in different kinds of effort:

  i) that which strives (contends) or fights
 ii) that which plays with
iii) that which submits to, yields to or indulges in something, which does not necessarily involve less exertion.

These are not exclusive attitudes. In some efforts we can

find both fighting against and indulgence in the task. But in all action there is some effort, physical and/or mental. 'Few people realize that their contentment in work and their happiness in life . . . is conditioned by the development and appropriate use of their individual efforts.'[8]

Collective action, Laban points out, is built up from mental and manual efforts of individuals. All our mental and physical exertion he saw as a combination, an interaction of: direction (space), rate (time) and dynamic (weight); in this interrelationship, each is influencing the others and being influenced by them in a variety of ways. (See Pattern 24 for detail.)

Pattern 23: Economy in Human Effort

The body needs to be used in the best way for each task. Every action should be executed with economy. Most people have to learn how to move without wasting their energies – which means finding the best starting position, then applying the appropriate amount of strength, employing the best use of space and moving at the appropriate pace. Different individuals will work at the same task in ways appropriate to them. Effective control of effort lies in a combination of the effort used and the individual applying it.

Pattern 24: Classification of Human Efforts

Study of the interaction of the basic elements in movement led Laban to identify eight basic working actions which in English came to be called the efforts.

Like other movements, efforts can be external or internal. Taking the two elements of each of the Motion factors – space, time and dynamic (weight), Laban identifies six elements:

- a movement can travel in space, either directly or indirectly
- a movement can involve time in either sustained or sudden ways
- a movement's dynamic or weight can be inclined towards lightness or heaviness.

These elements combine in eight different ways, and Laban identifies a basic effort action for each which he names according to its most generally recognized characteristic. All consciously performed functional activities can thus be broadly categorized:

- a light, indirect, sustained exertion – as in floating
- a light, direct, sustained exertion – as in gliding
- an indirect, sustained, strong exertion – as in wringing
- a sustained, strong, direct exertion – as in pressing
- a light, direct, quick exertion – as in dabbing
- an indirect, light, quick exertion – as in flicking
- a quick, strong, direct exertion – as in punching
- a strong, flexible, quick exertion – as in slashing.

Because of the continuous flux of human dynamics, the basic efforts are, of course, modified as any of the elements are adjusted.

Laban developed a number of diagrams showing the relationship between the efforts, grouping them into those which have one element in common, those which have two and those which because they are opposites, have none. This analysis gives a clearer understanding of the elements involved and the transitions which can follow.

Pattern 25: Effort and Recovery

'For man, the relationship of effort and recovery is one of the most important aspects of the great number of rhythmic alternations observable in Nature.'[9] Relaxation is the art of reducing tension. It might be total but can also refer to the act of becoming less rigid or of restoration after strain. It can refer to the release of one effort used and the move into a recovery period ready for the next effort.

Even the act of recovery requires some effort. So effort and recovery are not so much contrasts as opposites which do not exclude one another. Recovery is any means of restoring the inner balance; or, to put it another way, recovery takes place when the effort is directed towards inner healing rather than towards the outer world.

The flow of energy throughout life can be analysed as an effort rhythm.

Pattern 26: Rhythm

Rhythm, Laban defines as the 'alternation of opposite happenings' – organized tension and relaxation of tension – each with its own effort. Recognizing and establishing natural rhythms is a fundamental part of movement. He identifies three kinds of rhythm: natural, personal and occupational.

There is a fundamental alternation seen in that between work and sleep – though it has to be said that work is not exclusively effort and sleep is not exclusively recovery. The overall rhythm, however, is said to be a natural one since it follows the natural order of things seen in the earth's movement in relation to that of the sun and moon.

Each individual has an individual rhythm or pattern of rhythms and so responds to nutrition, reproduction, recreation, education and life's other activities with individuality. The variety of rhythms in man ranges from the simple to the complex.

The same kind of alternation is required throughout life and living: in the biological functioning of the body (its eating, gestation and disposal functions), in the mental, imaginative and emotional activity (intake of impressions, experiences, the sifting, sorting and assimilation of these and their reshaping in sleep or expression during waking hours).

Pattern 27: Balance

Balance is both an inner and an outer experience. It is achieved when the fight between the two extremes is resolved and equilibrium is restored. A well-proportioned alternation of rhythmic functions (light and strong, fighting and yielding) restores balance. The same basic scheme runs throughout all living matter, so that movement can be seen as man's link with the universal.

Pattern 28: Harmony

The concept of harmony appears throughout Laban's teaching and writing with varying shades of meaning: 'perfect co-ordination', 'equilibrium between forces pulling in opposite ways', 'a reconciliation of the forces within and without', 'a bringing together of tension and relaxation so as to effect that perfect balance', 'a uniting or re-uniting with the infinite', 'a reconciling of the internal with the external – and of the external with the infinite'.

Laban was interested in Pythagoras' discoveries in mathematics, especially the 'mathematics underlying musical scales',[10] leading to the belief that the same laws might exist in the heavens as in music. If number were the key to musical harmony, it might also be the key to the harmonies of the whole universe. In other words, there might also be a structural congruity between Man, his movement and the cosmos.

There are general harmonies which result from the structure of the body as well as harmonies which arise from both the physiological and the psychological individual state. In *Choreutics* Laban declares that 'an intensive study of the relationship between the architecture of the human body and its pathways in space facilitates the finding of harmonious patterns.' However, 'the shades and nuances of harmony elude ordinary verbal description', he maintains. 'We have to experience harmony in real bodily-mental participation.'[11] Movement is not just concerned with surface, tangible ends like getting from A to B, preparing a salad, making the bed, but it is also concerned with fitness, with satisfaction, with expression, with communication and with balance and co-ordination – the harmony of the whole human being.

Pattern 29: Space Harmony

Drawing together musical and mathematical (geometrical) terms and concepts, Laban proffers his idea of harmony of movement in space – the body co-operating with the patterns of nature in space. The simplest case of static space harmony is the body's symmetry. If we 'freeze' a movement we notice its form or shape. Movement is a continuity of forms travelling along certain paths.

> Dynamic symmetry arises, for instance, if the right side and the left side of the body are used successively as, say, in stepping or walking or any other form of locomotion. Space harmony in the deeper sense, however, is achieved only through an alternation of 'direct' and 'flexible' spatial effort qualities . . . In the behaviour of man, a whole scale of rhythms and harmonies can be observed. These range from the simplest . . . instinctive . . . to the most complex rhythms and harmonies of the rationally-experienced relationship between functions.[12]

Pattern 30: Scales

The anatomical structure of the body determines a series of natural sequences of movements which link different zones of the body and its limbs in a logical way. These identifiable movement sequences (which evolve naturally from the study of physical and mental functions, in everyday actions as well as dance) Laban, following the musical example, called scales.

'The wish to establish equilibrium through symmetric

movements is the simplest manifestation of what we call harmony; the aim of this is not simply to hold the body in an upright position, but to achieve a unity, a wholeness, a completeness.' It is the selection, order and relationship of movements in space which give the harmonic value: 'The integration of body and mind through movement occurs in the free performance of choreutic shapes. It is possible to construct a dynamic standard scale in which a chain of harmoniously linked emotions is related to a kinespheric movement path of the same shape.'[13]

Equilibrium through asymmetric movements has many aspects. The influence of flow which disturbs a simple symmetry leads to asymmetric movements which must necessarily be completed by other asymmetric tensions or moves.

The standard scale has two parts. The first series of six movements is situated in the opposite area of the Kinesphere from that of the second series of six movements. The inclination of the two series are parallel but they are followed in reversed direction. The standard scale, being the prototype of a chain which has equilibrium in its flow of forms, is the basis for the experience of spacial harmony. Used in training, these scales can help in the exploration and experience of harmony as well as assisting more generally the discovery of the body in space and space in the body.

Pattern 31: Geometric Shapes

Movement, of course, takes up all kinds of shapes, but by making reference to geometric forms Laban achieved two specific aims: (i) establishing a basic shape vocabulary which stimulates the imagination, and (ii) assisting further in the process of orientation – points for reference.

Plato's regular solids, circles, spirals, figures of eight and lines running in different directions are useful starting points for all kinds of movement composition and spur movement thinking and imagination. In all Laban's extant early drawings involving geometric shapes, one finds people moving amongst them. In the drawings which date from after the Second World War, the shift in emphasis is to the abstract. This seems also to have been a factor in his thinking. In the orientation of the body in space, the Kinesphere was established. To enable more specific reference points to be drawn, this sphere becomes simplified by reference to a number of geometric shapes within it. The cube serves as a useful initial shape enabling the individual to become aware especially of the dimensions of height, depth and breadth.

Pattern 32: The Icosahedron

Laban says in a revealing article in *LAMG Magazine* that early in his career he had observed 'that people, in spite of their differences of race and civilization, had something in common in their movement patterns'. When they were expressing emotion or excitement it became most obvious that they were, in their movement patterns, stressing certain points in space around the body. 'In joining these points,' he says, 'I arrived at a regular crystal form.'[14] This form he later identified as the icosahedron.

This was an exciting discovery for him since he had long wanted to associate man's movement possibilities with the crystalline structure and was delighted to be informed by a chemist that protein crystallizes in icosahedroid form.

'Man,' says Laban, 'is inclined to follow the connecting lines of the twelve corner points of an icosahedron with his movements in travelling as it were along an invisible network of paths,' and he goes on to point out that 'travelling along some of these paths produces harmonious and serene feelings and impressions while the following of other paths evokes feelings and impressions of anger, unhappiness and disharmony.'[15]

The icosahedron enables the detail of orientation to be

taken much further. The eight corners of the cube join the six square plane faces. To work with the three dimensions is to identify four rectangles, each with four corners, so giving twelve points in all touching the edge of the sphere. The faces between these form twenty equilateral triangles, making up the overall shape of the icosahedron. This is almost the sphere surrounding the space in which each individual can move and it provides an excellent means of recognizing and ordering directions used in human movement.

12 Social Ideas and Related Practice

Just as there is a general philosophy or world picture to Laban's discoveries about movement, there are also a number of social applications through which he practised his belief in the universality of movement.

Movement and Community – Choirs

From early days, Laban knew something of the value of movement as a corporate activity and went on to develop the idea of group work in movement into what he came to call the movement choir. He was, of course, taking up a practice in music but also following the ancient practice in Greek drama where there had been a group of performers, a chorus, who commented on the action through voice and movement.

Generally in singing and speaking choirs (both of which Laban used in his creative work), the participants gain their sense of togetherness by standing or sitting while the words and the sounds work together to give the sense of unity. In movement choirs, the participants become immersed in the flow of movement which forms the basis for their unity. As with a choir of voices, not all need be involved in the same way at the same time, so with the movement choir, groups may be subdivided, may work in unison or by contrast or through a variety of combinations of approaches.

The individual gains personal satisfaction in a social situation. Taking part in a movement choir helps each person to gain confidence through the group. Individuals take part who would never have thought of themselves as dancers. For many, their idea of a dancer had previously been of someone whose movement was light, flowing and upward. The movement choir enabled Laban to point out that just as not all singers have the vocal equipment to be soprano, so some dancers may by height and inclination be 'high', while others who are more earth bound tend to be 'low' and those who work more comfortably somewhere in between are 'middle' dancers. Through the movement choirs, many have re-educated their sense of rhythm and flow and discovered the pleasures of expressive movement.

Movement and Society – Celebration and Festival

Society, like the individual, needs to live with rhythm. Communally, as well as individually, we have our times of effort and stress so we also need our times of relaxation and release of tension. Laban recognized two kinds of festival:

- those which are organized to help us cope with loss or great change (often with a religious side)
- those which celebrate some culmination in the world of work.

Amongst the festivals in the first group Laban points out what an illuminating and satisfying experience dance can be when performed at a funeral or a wedding or an anniversary, especially when it draws upon the natural movement patterns of the society which it serves. It was the repetition of effort patterns common to a community that he recognized as forming the basis of tribal and national dances.

Festivals arising from work celebrate the day-to-day breadwinning activities of industry and commerce. Laban organized several of these, notably the great Trades Festival in Vienna in 1929. It was a twentieth-century equivalent of the medieval guild pageants. Each of the trades of industries had its waggon or float and presented, in movement and dance, aspects of their crafts and profession. Four hundred different 'stages' brought together blacksmiths, bakers, printers and paper manufacturers, carpenters and decorators, gardeners and laundry-workers, tailors, telephonists and tinsmiths, undertakers and umbrella makers, watchmakers and weavers. Each using their different work rhythms and space patterns, they combined and consolidated their efforts in a celebration of the achievements of the whole city.

Festivals, Laban insists, are not only important in the overall rhythm of effort and recovery, but play an important part in re-establishing pride in and loyalty to work, community spirit and an overall sense of achievement and spiritual well-being.

The Status of Dance – Union and Congress

For all his romanticism, Laban showed a surprising sense of practical awareness. Brought up in the belief that he was a member of the ruling class, he never lost the common touch and seeing his profession regarded so poorly made him all the more determined to change things.

Not only were dancers as a profession regarded as only a little above prostitutes, they also had no means of exerting influence in the way that other occupations (deemed to be more necessary) often did. Laban could see that the greatest strength came through unity and as early as his Paris days he had attempted to establish an Artists' Colony. Finally in 1927 he organized the First German Dance Congress. By this time those in classical ballet already had an organization and Laban, Jooss and others brought together all dancers of every persuasion, style or technique and managed to persuade them to unify in the German Dance League. It was a tremendous achievement, not only because it made people notice that dance was a worthy art form but also because the

Congress was a forum for the sharing of findings and the dissemination of ideas.

An Enduring Art Form – Dance Writing

Festivals, large and small, movement choirs, educational work in schools and colleges and later work improvement in factories and offices, together with movement therapy, became easier with the introduction of kinetography or movement notation. Never before had the art of dance possessed such a universal set of symbols for recording its endeavours. With his invention of what has become known as Labanotation, Laban had achieved that ambition of putting dance alongside literature and music with a notation all its own.

Even today, with the greater access of film and the ever-readiness of video, Laban's notation remains as important as written forms in other arts. Dance, he knew had to be seen to be more than ephemeral. At a dance performance, there is no opportunity for contemplation – the spectator's mind is forcibly submerged by the flow of ever-changing happenings.

Building on earlier attempts, Laban, with his colleagues, had worked out something far more comprehensive, far more flexible. Labanotation uses a three-line staff, the central line of which is related to the central line of the body. The lines run vertically and the notation is read from the base to the top following the line of movement. The central line also provides the timing and is marked (like music) with beats and bars. The notes or blocks on the lines are shaped to indicate the direction of movement. Solid black dots or stripes indicate the level (low, middle or high); the time the movement takes is indicated by the length of the symbol (longer, slower; shorter, faster). The position of the symbol on the staff indicates which part of the body, while other symbols modify the main structure of the movement.

It remains remarkable not just because it means that any or all movement can be written down, but because it firmly established Laban's insistence that movement is a language whose symbols need to be no less limited or limiting than those recording verbal monologue or thought. Once its basic principles have been mastered, it can be used anywhere for any conceivable kind of human activity.

Part Five

TURNING THEORY INTO PRACTICE

'. . . he had his ideas . . . and it was then for other people to carry on . . .'

John Martin, former *New York Times* dance critic.

Turning Theory into Practice

Laban's ideas, his theory and principles, are so fundamental that there is hardly any part of life to which some aspects of them cannot be applied. In some areas, notable pioneers and scholars have already taken his ideas and extended their application to points beyond those he had reached by the end of his life.

Laban had been developing his theory and principles for well over thirty years, so it was easy enough for him, during the last twenty years of his life, to apply them to any of the diverse activities that were demanded of him. And he clearly did it all with great success. Only in the more abstract aspects of his work, however, did he write about it. More often, Laban simply referred to the basics, or indicated first principles, pointing the directions – then he left us to find our own way.

Not surprisingly, many people have experienced difficulty in applying his theory for themselves, feeling unable to identify a secure enough foundation from which to proceed. The foregoing clarification of the basic patterns should go some way to supplying a foundation on which to build a process of putting Laban theory to practical use today. It is, however, not a mechanical process. Laban, we have seen, has not provided a formula, or even a method. The principles and patterns which arise from his theory depend for their effectiveness in application on each individual's resourcefulness and creativity. Knowledge and understanding of Laban patterns have to be accompanied by imagination and vision.

At first the task may seem daunting but once the initial reluctance can be overcome, it is less perplexing and the whole value of Laban's work is far more evident.

The aim here is to help start this process for anyone willing to begin mastering movement. This section in no way aims to be prescriptive or exhaustive; it seeks only to give pointers, to initiate ideas and to stimulate imagination so that anyone can begin applying Laban's ideas to a field (or fields) of interest. Neither the areas chosen here nor their treatment in the terms suggested are exclusive. Suggestions in one section might well be appropriate to, or modified for, another. Whole books could be (and in some cases, have been) written on these and other topics. The following are offered as examples (arranged in what could be a progressional sequence) to animate movement imagination and excite further thought, enquiry and experimentation.

The basic principle throughout is: 'play' with the ideas; that is, experiment, improvise, try out different things in different ways.

Each of the 32 patterns mentioned here can be taken and explored by using any of the other patterns. Pattern 1, for example, can be tested through observation, through imitation, through abstracting any number of space, weight, dynamic or effort qualities and recreating them in movement. At the other end, Pattern 32, for instance, can be used as stimulus for improvisations with different parts of the body starting from different points of the icosahedron. Various planes can be linked with other planes through other geometric shapes, with a variety of directions, timings and dynamics. The possibilities are endless.

13   Preparatory Process –
Acquiring Preliminary Skills

(See also Patterns 7, 8, 17–22; Ch. 6, *Modern Educational Dance*; Ch. 7, *Effort*)

It would be as well to begin by developing what have been referred to as 'the tools for the discovery of movement'. Following Laban's own example, train the eye by observing movement – everywhere: in buses, trains, cars, restaurants, shops, in the factory, office, street and any place where there are people. Begin with general observations and gradually home into details. Similarly, observe movement on different occasions: people at work, involved in all kinds of recreation and festivity or simply in their everyday activities of eating, travelling and going about their usual round.

Become fascinated by the way people walk, talk, stand, sit, lift, push, pass, avoid, greet, meet and generally relate to one another. Notice what they do with their hands, their feet, their shoulders, their spinal columns. Observe whole body movements and shadow movements. What are the different impressions which they make on you/others? How does the movement seem to affect the mind (mirrored in the face) and vice versa? How far does movement seem to be indicative of the inner state of being?

Then begin the process of analysis by asking why and how these impressions are made. What parts of the body are involved and in what ways? What kinds (qualities) of movement result? Are these conscious, open movements or are they shadow movements, more related to the habitual and the unconscious? What are the needs being satisfied?

Make notes, sketches and diagrams to help retain and recall movements. Acquire some fundamental knowledge and understanding of Labanotation (see, for example, *Practical Kinetography Laban* by Valerie Preston-Dunlop). Single out specific moments to consider these in greater detail.

Tape documentaries and other TV programmes and play short sequences back until you begin to recognize statements people are making with their body language. Use a video camera to film sequences of others and play back certain (however ordinary) movement sequences many times over, so that things missed at first can be examined in more detail later. Compare these with your notation.

Similarly, video sequences of yourself doing various tasks and look thoughtfully at your own movement patterns. Throughout, look with an understanding rather than a critical eye. Ask why and what causes this or that movement. Aim to be an objective observer, one who is keen to notice just what is happening and why; what is involved and how, rather than only commenting on how 'good' or 'bad' it looks at first glance. Train the memory to hold on to some of these images and from time to time test quality of recall against a video recording, notation or detailed notes.

Finally, observation, analysis and memory can be used to create new ways of doing things. Experiment. Make up fresh sequences, both specific and abstract developed out of work, social and recreational patterns.

With this background, it should be possible to take on the idea of 'thinking in terms of movement'. Our logic suggests that we then apply Laban's principles to training of the instrument itself – the body. It is our means of making sense of the world, our total and only means of experience and expression. It is the basis for all other areas of application. The body must be fit, healthy, poised and ready for action.

14 The Body – Its Fitness and Health

(See also Patterns 10–12, 16–28; sections in *The Dancer's World, Mastery of Movement on the Stage*)

Laban's ideas and discoveries are basic to understanding the body, to maintaining its general health and to keeping it functioning finely with sense and sensitivity. Fitness and health lie at the foundation of any and all other applications of Laban's ideas. Until the instrument is in good order, it will not be able to respond adequately to the application of his ideas in other fields.

Fitness, for Laban, is not the end in itself but the means towards fuller living, expressing and communicating. His is a holistic approach, recognizing the interrelationship of the inner and outer both from the point of view of the physical and the psychological – 'the unitary function of body and mind'. His emphasis upon balance and harmony provides the ultimate aim and gives a framework in which all activities can be monitored.

Posture

Fitness begins with posture. The human being stands upright, against the gravitational pull, and needs to learn how to control and harness the tensions which result from this conflict. Balance and harmony should be the keynote to good stance, as elsewhere. Recognizing the structure of the body and working always with a regard for its symmetry, individual posture is a prime consideration and the basis for all activity. It is the key to any sense of well-being.

Work for easy alignment. Imagine a line gently drawing the head upwards, keep the trunk balanced above the pelvis and the pelvis poised above the feet. Check this balance by standing with your heels about a couple of inches from the wall (feet about 18" apart). Keeping the toes on the ground, gradually take your body back against the wall. Aim to let the shoulder blades and buttocks touch the wall together. Reduce the gap between the small of the back and the wall by bending both knees. Hold this position for a while.

A similar approach can be taken by lying with your back on the floor and knees bent, hands by your sides. Slowly release first one leg, then the other and feel how with time and practice the spinal column begins to lie flat along the floor. Use this awareness of posture and alignment as you stand, sit and move around.

A straight but flexible spine, strong, flat abdominal wall and an upright head (neck free from tensions) should be worked for in such a way that once more, the neutral poise and balanced posture actually feel quite 'natural'.

Following each area mentioned in Pattern 16, use: stretching, swinging, pressing, pulling, turning, twisting. Explore different ways of working the spine, e.g. bending, stretching, turning, twisting in all directions and from different starting positions: e.g. lying down on the front, on the back, sitting on the floor, on a bench, curling up, rocking back and forwards on the spinal column. Begin gently and grade the complexity.

Bad posture can be corrected and muscles strengthened and toned up. Then, once achieved, good posture has to be maintained. Bad habits lead to severe physical (and mental) problems; whereas good habits of movement aid the general sense of well-being. We appear old because we stoop – we do not need to stoop because we are old.

Once you begin to feel a sense of balance in the body,

explore ways of sitting, lying down, getting up, which help maintain the balance and avoid undue strain. Keep the trunk weight over the pelvis and bring the pelvis over the feet. 'Play' with easy turns and twists so that no matter what positions the body moves into, poise and equilibrium can be restored easily and naturally.

Relaxation

Aim to release unnecessary tension when standing against a flat surface such as the plain wall, or lying face upwards, spinal column against the floor. Consciously taking concentration through every part of the body, 'let go' tensions to restore a natural equilibrium based on the body's symmetry. Like all exercises, it should be a mental and physical activity.

Done well, the act of relaxation not only releases the stress but restores the energy in the rhythm of effort and recovery (cf. Patterns 19–21, 23 and 24).

Correction

Using observation and awareness, get to know the body. Check out where the points of imbalance are, where the alignment is out of harmony and where the hyper-tensions most easily collect. Check this in a variety of 'still' positions (standing, sitting, lying). Release the unnecessary tensions (mind over matter), straighten the spine and correct the symmetry and balance. The fact that improved posture noticeably develops the sense of well-being is usually the incentive needed to maintain a vigilance and sustain the 'natural' poise.

Breathing

Focus on the centre of gravity and feel the source of inner energy which can build and grow from here. Work on the breathing, using the outward expansion of the lower ribs (from the end of the breast bone to the lower tip of the rib cage). Most people use only shallow breathing and at first find they have little outward and upward expansion of the lower ribs.

Seek to gain control of the breathing (both intake and exhalation) through regular practice. Keep aware of its rhythm and depth of flow. Never allow any exercise to become merely mechanical. Ensure good breathing with the body in varying positions. Aim to avoid cramping the abdominal area; keep the lower ribs free for expansion. Explore changing rhythms in breathing and the overall effect on the body.

With good posture and good breathing, the next focus is to ensure that all aspects of the body remain in good working order.

Clear Objectives

Every physical workout should have its two-way effects and should be contributing to overall confidence and contentment. At every stage, fitness and health are functional.

In working out a programme based on Laban principles of harmony and balance as part of the unitary function of body and mind there are a number of pointers to aim for:

- Flexibility – using the ideas of the body in space and working so that every area of the trunk, limbs, neck and head acquires and maintains suppleness.
- Strength – awareness of Laban's motion factors means exploring movement qualities, using appropriate tension to keep muscles and limbs strong as well as flexible. Be aware of the tensions brought into play by working against the body's own weight as well as the weight/ weights (or other resistance) outside it.
- Stamina – building strong, flexible breathing throughout the exercise helps develop endurance and stamina, strengthening the heart, encouraging good blood flow, gradually creating greater, easier endurance.

- Centring – keeping an awareness of the centre of gravity, good posture and confident movement helps to maintain a flow of energy and presence, building towards:
- Economy of effort, control and coordination – it is not enough merely to exercise the body; it is the manner in which the exercises are carried out that builds health and fitness in the Laban sense. Having discovered, therefore, where there are unnecessary tensions, focus on releasing those parts of the body from undue effort. Explore the ways in which natural rhythm helps the economy and strengthens the coordination.

All this exploration can be given variety (both for general interest and overall balance) through exercises devised from the imaginative use of Laban's understanding of space, weight, time and flow. Be especially aware that twisting and turning movements are good, as well as those which work in straight lines. Here, each individual expands consciousness of the range between the extremes of violent and delicate action, rapid and sustained motion, as part of developing a spatial awareness and general personal assurance.

Such an approach prevents over-emphasis in any one area, direction or dynamic and is a challenge to conventional 'keep-fit' or the uniformity of dynamic found in say, aerobics or Yoga. 'Playing with' the elements makes exercise more experimental, more creative (use both abstract ideas and specific, everyday situations), and emphasizes mental and emotional involvement alongside the physical.

- Rhythms – whether working with or without music or sound accompaniment, vary the beat. Sustain some exercises, speed up others. Feel the pleasure of repetition, of progression and of variety.
- Fit for life – the test of fitness is not seen simply in appearance or the feel-good factor, but should be evident in day-to-day activity. All that control, co-ordination and effort economy should be seen in the way in which we use the body as it carries out its various tasks. The training gives greater awareness of such aspects as natural rhythm, weight management and spatial relationships.
  It should be evident especially in how we stand and sit while carrying out and engage in, all kinds of activities. It should

be manifest in the way we handle, push, pull, or lift things ensuring the best relationship of the object to the body and the body to the task undertaken, whether preparing a meal, word-processing or moving a heavy box from the floor to a shelf.

The body must of course be nourished by good food. Like the rest of the human organism, the digestive, excretory and circulatory systems are subject to the same movement factors. The intake of food has to be nourishing to provide the resources that fuel the body and here as elsewhere the balance provided by variety of texture (strength), directness and indirectness and flow, all play their part. Chemical action and reaction must work alongside the movement qualities. At all times, the movement of solids and liquids goes on so that the individual needs to be aware of allowing plenty of space around the abdomen as well as helping the action to continue through external physical movement.

Bodily fitness becomes a means by which it is possible to relate more effectively to one's environment, other people and the situations life has to offer.

15 The Voice – Its Fitness and Health

(See also Patterns 7, 11, 12, 16–26; sections in *The Dancer's World, Mastery of Movement on the Stage*)

Though we often speak and think of it separately, Laban reminds us the voice is, like the rest of the living body, expressed through movement. Speech is a further manifestation of the body's activity. It is expression and communication.

Voice consists of breath vibrating past the vocal chords and articulated into speech by movement of the organs in the mouth. Vocal fitness has its foundations in bodily posture, flexible use of the lower ribs to allow the base of the lungs to expand, and a strong abdominal wall for support. Good use of tension and relaxation is vital throughout.

Observation, analysis, memory and imagination are again crucial; this time, employing both eye and ear; the eye will look for posture and visible functions of the trunk, while the ear needs to observe the sounds, their quality and effect. Use any or all of the ideas in Chapter 13 in relation to sound. Observe people talking on all kinds of occasions and in a variety of situations. Listen to voices that squeeze out of narrow spaces, open up into large space, sound strong or weak, indulge in time or appear to have no time to spare, weave in space or more directly in space, and so forth. Notice the effects these have on you and others. Which are easy on the ear, which hard to listen to? Then continue further analysis by noting which sounds are clear, which maintain interest and give a range of expression and why? With free-flowing movement comes a liberation of the voice and a natural desire for speech. Tongue-tied people tend first of all to be physically inhibited; releasing the body and giving it a confidence in rhythm and flow is a good beginning for closer attention to the voice.

Once good habits of breathing have been established, there can be greater concentration on flexibility and expansion of the lower ribs and lungs. For speech and good vocal tone, control ensures that the speaker never needs to 'run out of breath'. This involves good co-ordination so that intake of breath can be snatched quickly and the exhalation of the column of air along the windpipe to the cavities of the mouth, sustained and prolonged as necessary. It is here that Laban's principles of the two-way process – mind with body/ body with mind – again come into their own. Breath is placed forward in the mouth to ensure good resonance and this is a mental guiding of the process: 'thinking' the voice forward onto the hard palate.

Because most of the time we speak quite quickly, the organs of articulation (tongue, teeth, lips, jaw, hard and soft palates) have to be kept flexible, so once more it is possible to 'play with' putting the mouth into all kinds of shapes and with a variety of efforts. Each articulative organ can be explored separately. Then two can be taken together and all kinds of sounds created. Speech is made up of vocalized breath given free flow (vowels) and that which is bound or stopped (consonants). It is awareness of breath in space outside the body which helps the projection of the voice and awareness of space within the body (changing the space within the mouth as we reshape it) which helps clear enunciation. This awareness changes the pitch and allows it to glide from one height or depth to another in its inflections.

The pace or rate of utterance is simply the application of Laban's principle of time and the understanding of weight or quality which gives speech its dynamic. Playing with all kinds of stress on syllables, words and phrases can add to the whole colour in communication.

Likewise with other principles: rhythm, pattern, flow (which controls phrasing) can each be experimented with to observe effect and implement their part in effective use of that wonderful instrument of oral transmission.

Being in harmony with one's body and voice is the way to use the instrument to its fullest advantage. A recent survey suggested that 80% of job offers came as a result not of what was said so much as how it was said. A well-used voice makes its impact on the listener's conscious and unconscious mind.

So-called 'defects of speech' can also be understood in the light of Laban's principles. Usually they can be analysed into problems of tension, flexibility, controllability, flow and rhythm. Accents, dialects and other variations of the spoken norms can also be understood by observation along similar lines, especially when looked at from the principles of space, time and dynamic. Patterns of factors which affect movement naturally also play a part in affecting speech.

Even though it is necessary from time to time to concentrate upon voice and speech, sound progress will only be made and a healthy instrument maintained if we never lose sight of the fact that this is not a throat and mouth speciality. We are not 'talking heads', but hopefully working as individual personalities – the body communicates holistically.

With the body and voice fit and ready, we can begin applying Laban's patterns to other ways in which we relate to the world.

16   Education, Experience and Expression

(See also Patterns 7, 8, 11, 13, 15, 21–27; *Gymnastics and Dance, Modern Educational Dance*)

The application of Laban's principles throughout education grows logically from his findings that movement of the body is our only way of discovering ourselves and our environment as well as our means of releasing, recreating and communicating ideas and feelings. What better foundation for education?

Soon after the Second World War, a white paper, 'Educational Reconstruction', maintained that primary education should foster 'the potentialities of children' whose minds are 'nimble and receptive, their curiosity strong, their imagination fertile and their spirits high'. The curriculum, it went on, 'is too often cramped and distorted by overemphasis on examination subjects and on ways and means of defeating the examiners'.[1] It is still true, but in our anxiety for tangible results we quickly lose sight of it.

Because Laban's own experience had informed him better than his school instructors, he realized that, especially in the early years of childhood, it was easy to have too much adult interference, where often free exploration was more productive. In those early years we learn better from doing for ourselves, gaining direct experience of the world and thinking about it. Then we want to give form to feeling through all kinds of expression. An excellent principle throughout is that of exploring, experimenting, once more, 'playing' on a physical, mental and emotional level. The implications are there for the learning environment which needs its sense of space, time and dynamic (quality/weight).

In *Children's Gymnastics and Dance* he had identified four stages of growth: pre-school, schooldays, adolescence and a period of developing sexual maturity. These are not simply physical-education phases of progression but, remembering the holistic approach, also related to the mental, emotional and spiritual aspects. All facets are interconnected: movement affects body, mind and spirit; mind and spirit affect the body and its movement.

We are limiting our experience through education when we neglect the central position of movement: doing. Like all other aspects of living, education demands constant awareness of the physical. A body which is inhibited and afraid will not be receptive to learning.

Even when we are sitting or standing, apparently passively, the bodily position is important because it is related to the mental. A person sitting slumped over a desk is less receptive, less 'actively' involved than a person sitting leaning towards the material or the teacher. An alert body helps maintain an alert mind. Laban's principles applied to education, however, mean less sitting at desks and more free-range activity – not because it seems 'liberal' and avant-garde, but because that is the way we gain our understanding and our self-confidence. Physical release helps liberate the whole personality. We have grown to deplore hens being kept and fed in battery conditions, yet all too often we seem to believe that knowledge and understanding should be fed to children and adults by keeping them sitting in rows for long parts of each day. Not everyone might feel inspired to arrange the whole of the curriculum around specific 'movement' activities throughout education but, if we follow Laban, activity must be both physical and mental unless we seek to deny the very nature of the human animal.

At least one head teacher did have the courage to give a

movement core to the entire school programme within his Birmingham primary school, counteracting the wartime years and conditions. Mr L. A. Stone took over the headship of Steward Street Junior School shortly after the outbreak of the Second World War. He was a teacher who was willing to experiment and one who illustrated Laban's educational aspirations when he declared 'we were trying to give the children the freedom which could break down the inhibitions already developed, freedom which could enable them to go ahead and do those things which would be best for their own development. 'For a child to be free', he asserts, 'the first essential is that he should move easily.' He sought to release confidence, interest and concentration, to inculcate self-discipline, and encourage freedom from fear.

The key to such personal development (as well as to the development of the arts throughout the school) he saw to be movement and this idea gained further credence when two of his teachers returned to the school having taken a course in 'Modern Dance'. The dance course had to have been run by Laban-trained people at this point in English Educational practice, and the one his teachers undertook was most likely conducted by Lisa Ullmann.

Those children under Mr Stone's care gained their experience and understanding through movement activities and used movement and dance to give their ideas expression. They found that making their own rhythms and movement patterns was an excellent foundation for more formal activities such as folk dance, skipping, running and so on. They learned balance, discovered space, explored time and 'played with' different movement qualities. Soon Laban ideas of effort-training took effect and the children gained more confidence and freedom as they began to explore their own effort patterns. They 'made their own patterns in the space about them as dictated by the individual ideas they wished to express.'

Observing the youngsters in his school, Mr Stone, in true

Laban form, made his own discovery about the arts as a whole. 'Soon it became obvious that the creative urge expressed in all the arts comes from the same source,' he says. The expression may be different but it springs from a common denominator. 'That common beginning,' Stone confirms, 'is movement.'[2]

This experience fed into the children's painting, their modelling, their skill and bodily strengthening in PE, their expression of feeling and idea in dance and their articulation through drama. An additional value lay in the fact that dance and drama activities bring experience together in a tangible end product involving the whole person.

The results were incredible, creating a vibrant sense of community throughout the school. Children were more open and socially adept as well as displaying higher standards of general academic attainment. Mime led naturally to the spoken word and because it was their language expressing their feelings and ideas, they tended to speak it with clarity and good enunciation. Then the speeches were written down and their English work began to develop. Acting out a story led to wanting to read it and re-use the language and ideas it contained. Most children began to become easily involved with painting and awareness of space and pattern led to greater sense of shape in art work generally. Flow and rhythm seemed to transfer naturally from their movement to their art and from their art into their handwriting and composition. What a foundation for those children and what an example for some of our ethnically mixed schools of today.

Laban principles are just as sound at every other stage of education. When we merely concentrate on the cerebral aspect of learning we miss the full benefits. A balance must be struck.

Mental as well as physical tensions need releasing and throughout the learning process we can keep in mind the rhythm of effort and recovery. Working within a natural rhythm of activities (drawing on contrasting efforts, mental as well as physical, some light, some strong, some direct, some indirect, and so on), helps to make the whole of educational development far more effective. What we have experienced as a whole, united individual, tends to remain with us in a way that rote-learning never can.

Laban's own approach provides some good precepts for teachers: observe what is happening and analyse it. Raise questions rather than supply answers. See what the students have to offer and build from there rather than superimposing an overprepared scheme and then wanting to instruct it. Lead the students in the search for knowledge. Improvise and explore different approaches so that the students find their own interest and absorption.

Good education is a cyclical process. It is not enough to gain experience, knowledge, understanding and so on: what we have taken in, we need to release. Without adequate expression, all the intake in the world will do no one any good – at worst, it will find its own outlet in destructive tendencies. Education can provide opportunities for, and skill in, creative, constructive outlets. This physical/mental approach demands and inculcates a self-disciplined attitude and sets up patterns and principles which, like all true education, form a sound foundation for life.

Amongst those foundations, building relationships on Laban principles is a great help in understanding others and even in relating to them in the most intimate of ways.

17   Lovemaking and Sex

(See also Patterns 9, 10, 14, 15–19, 23–26)

Sex is the great art not just of moving but of touching, positioning, responding and relating to another individual. So all those Laban patterns about space, time (and timing) and weight (quality) are applicable and, here as elsewhere, give stimulus to greater expression and experience.

A phrase in common use is 'love-play', underlining the 'playing with' attitude to movement. Lovemaking and sex can be undertaken in an inventive, imaginative way, making the interrelationship a creative, shared experience. Awareness of Laban patterns enables an extension of ideas and gives a framework for introspection and discussion.

Very often movement is for the doer; in loveplay and sex, the movement is also (or more so) for the partner. The quality of the sexual experience comes from the co-operating, the collaborating and the one-to-one sharing. Making love usually involves two compatible individuals relating intimately through body, mind and feeling. At its best it becomes a kind of improvised dance in which the dancers grow in sensitivity to one another.

Lovers, like dancers, explore space, movement quality and time. Partners, each in their own space, begin to move as one. Their movements might start with attitude and gesture, go from hands touching to the caress, and proceed gradually to the most central of all movements, performed and experienced through the mystery of intercourse. Through-out, their physical response is governed by the interrelation between their inner and outer experience. Internal feeling stimulates and motivates the external physical movement and vice versa.

Degrees of tension alternate with varying degrees of relaxation as each responds to the other. Rhythms are established and combine. Together they adjust, creating new rhythms which inform them, revealing to themselves their positive emotions and harmonious qualities as well as perhaps discovering negative feelings of remoteness and discord.

Sex can bring its role-play too. There might be moments when one initiates and leads, the other following, times when roles reverse or merge, slowly evolve or change suddenly each one introducing a new dynamic pattern, creating another space, timing and rhythm. The body language and movement are subconsciously echoing the 'free' and 'bound' flow, the quality and basic efforts identified by Laban.

Relating understanding of Laban to the experience of making love should confirm the realization that its possibilities are infinite and this emotional, physical, mental, spiritual activity is yet one further means by which we can gain insight into the mystery of ourselves and those who are near and dear to us. Above all, it should remind us of the unified nature of the human being and its experience.

The body is the sole expressive instrument in two other major art forms: dancing and acting. Because of their different points of focus, each calls for different points of emphasis in bodily expression. Dancing uses all the body (but not usually the voice) to express ideas, feeling, shapes, patterns.

Because of the size of its gestures and movements, it focuses best on the abstract or the abstracted while drama, which also involves the whole body (and the voice), deals more readily with the concrete, the real, the specific situation. In dance-drama the two arts combine. Both draw from keen observation but their 'imitation' of nature is resourceful and creative.

18 Dance

(See also Patterns 15–32; *The Dancer's World*; *Mastery of Movement on the Stage*; and Laban's own dance practice seen through Wigman, Bereska and Jooss – see Chapter 7)

The dancer was foremost in Laban's mind throughout his working life, though especially in his thinking and practice before 1938. It was his investigations into the world of the dancer which led him to discover the bases of movement which can be applied elsewhere. Almost anything and everything he discovered can be utilized by the dancer.

With Laban, dance training involves mind and spirit as well as body, so classwork, discussion, experimental workshops, rehearsal and performance proceed as part of the process in which one of the aims is to liberate the individual as an artist and help him or her discover that artistry. The Laban dancer knows the instrument and how it works, but this instrument is never just the physical body trained through techniques in isolation. The well-tuned instrument is crucial, but with it the dancer learns how to be more fully expressive and acquires the language which helps to extend the movement thinking and creativity. Laban set out to open up physical expression. Vocabulary and syntax develop into the expressive communication of the dance. The training grows on the foundations of, and the frequent reference to, rhythm, balance and harmony.

Many content themselves simply with the skills – acquiring, through regular practice, a given set of agilities which

can be drawn upon in developing a choreography. Laban
demands a fresh look at what is meant by technique. His
practice and ideas suggest a broad and more flexible
approach. With Laban, dance training is more a matter of
inexhaustible exploration, the kind of technique-training
which allows individuality and from which the dancer can
make his/her own way. No less disciplined, skilled or
rigorous, though different in its demands. His dance
language is not based upon limited, learnt particulars but
upon principles which enable the individual to develop an
extensive and infinitely variable vocabulary, capable of a vast
range of contributions to choreographic communication.

Mary Wigman is the supreme example of the dancer
trained on Laban's principles. She illustrates the aims and
aspirations of Laban's 'new dance', acknowledging the body
in its truth together with the sharpness and clarity of a strong
mind. A new spontaneity and dynamic quality are evident.

Dance, on Laban's principles, is not just the body in poses
with variations. There is also emphasis on flow and
uninhibited gesture. The motivating power for the dance
movement comes from within, is life-demanding and
employs the whole being. It is dance not as it has been but as
it might become, communicating richness and power and
taking an audience to where the physical existence reaches
towards Laban's cosmic world.

Dance is about relationships – the relationship of the
individual to space itself and to other individuals in that
space and dance training aims to discover and utilize these.

All Laban's explorations in space patterns are pertinent
for the dancer, together with that awareness of time and
quality, when and how to move in executing the patterns.
And this is an internal as well as an external response, the
quality of movement and its rhythmic expression being
communicated from an inner sensation through an instrument attuned to the moment. The dancer moves confidently
in all directions. The aim is to explore the full range of

possibilities of the dancer's posture and gesture by utilizing all the planes and employing the three-dimensional nature of dance. It is a disciplined training but one that ultimately leads to greater freedom and a more creative, expansive approach.

While recognizing the validity of the classical tradition, Laban was always keen to extend the dancer's range in other areas, such as the dynamic, the time and rhythm. His principles are not at odds with the classical ballet, but simply by opening up its techniques, takes the concepts further. His thinking easily takes on board such elements of technique as the five foot positions or the '*port de bras*', but, starting more basically by exploring direction and expansion into the three planes, helps dancers to become more aware of further possibilities and the principles underlying them. What Laban does is to take the emphasis away from decoration to emphasize expression and to provide the dancer with a framework or context within which the discipline is released into greater creativity and freedom.

Within his broadly holistic concern, at times experience and dexterity can be further extended by focusing on detail through different Laban patterns or principles. Every limb, every aspect of the dancer has to learn to communicate with vividness. As a dancer himself, Laban dazzled even those close to him with certain aspects of his expressive power. Jooss said of his hands that it was 'as if fire came from them when they were in motion'. According to Wigman, Laban 'is the only and great experimenter with the dance'; so Laban's approach is by 'playing', exploring, studying each part of the dancer's vocabulary, including:

- movements of different parts of the body (head, shoulders, arms, hands and so on), into the space, discovering what they can do, where they can go and how far and with what qualities (lighter or stronger)
- leaps and jumps, turns and twists, rolls and falls – again into the space from a variety of starting positions
- relationships, pair work, work in threes and other small

groups – working close or far, in open or closed attitudes
- proximity, contact with different parts of the body and different qualities of touch, weight-bearing, rhythms of all kinds specific effort shapes, dimensions, planes, directions and other patterns – here too changing the dynamic throughout the studies
- varying qualities of lightness and strength, flow, tension and the like – in relation to all the experimentation
- styles, the expressive, the tragic, the comic, the stylized, free form, burlesque, cabaret, folk – everything can be played in different ways.

Such explorations assist kinaesthetic awareness and, used creatively, further extend the overall range of abstract expressive communication. At other times the focus is on the use of this detail in the shaped and developed dance.

The dancer can explore myth, symbol, pattern, drama, themes of all kinds (social, religious, abstract, concrete, human aspirations or vices, natural or supernatural) in developing a dance. Dances can take on major themes (like the Big City, Dances of Life, Dances of Death, War, Tyranny, The Homeless) or lighter subjects (like Carnival, Rhythm, Magicians, Light, Dream Birds).

Laban principles liberate the choreographer too. Jooss is the student of his who gained most fame and international recognition as a choreographer but it is as well to remember that Laban himself choreographed, with Toscanini as conductor and Siegfried Wagner directing at the festivals at Bayreuth. For four years he was choreographing at the Berlin State Opera. Following Noverre, he stressed the ultimate seriousness of purpose in the dance but maintained that there is no theme or subject that cannot be taken on and expressed through dance. Likewise, for him there is no genre or style through which it cannot work whether it be comic or tragic, stylized or freeform, formal, abstract or theatrical dance-drama.

Having trained his dancers to be creative, he preferred to choreograph with and from this creativity. Laban was a master of improvisation and that is how most of his choreography was carried out. First, he stimulated dancers' ideas of movement, getting them to experiment and try things out. When he sensed the time was right, he would select sequences and then shape them skilfully, sometimes brilliantly, into the final dance structure. Rehearsals were just as important a part of the developmental process as were classes and workshops.

This was the way he built a genuine company, without 'stars' or a *corps de ballet*. The emphasis was on the dancers themselves, so that décor and costume were there to work with the choreography. He delighted in bringing the arts together and often pioneered dance performed with varying aural accompaniment: in silence, with simple percussion, with human voice, the spoken or sung sound, solo or full choir, with piano(s) or full orchestra. Every moment had to be a telling expressive moment in the overall concept.

Working as an ensemble, without 'stars', enables the whole company to discover the rhythms within a dance and to communicate them together. Exploring simple settings and telling props and costumes helps additionally to establish the focus on the dancer and his/her communicative skills.

Based on Laban principles and practice, choreography can show the dance liberated from rigid technical language. Not employing formal steps or standard poses, choreography on Laban principles, no matter what its genre or structure, seeks continually to explore the essence and meaning of movement itself.

19   Drama

(See also Patterns 7 & 8, 10, 12, 21–27, 31 and 32; *Mastery of Movement on the Stage* and *Movement Psychology*)

Laban's ideas can be applied to the directing and mounting of the play and to the training and preparation of the actor as himself or in building the role.

Before arriving in England, Laban's acting experience was largely through dance-drama. According to Joan Littlewood, he had watched Stanislavski rehearsing once in Berlin but was not impressed. In fact, he told her, he found the experience rather boring. When the Second World War was over he had the opportunity to develop his own theory and practice in the UK.

'Human movement, with all its physical, emotional and mental implications, is the common denominator of the dynamic art of the theatre.'[3] The actor talks with his body – not just the vocal apparatus within the body but the body as a whole. Every aspect of his body language is capable of a wide range of subtlety of communication. The actor has to know what he wants to say and how he wants to say it.

It is possible to identify three aspects of the Laban training process particularly appropriate for actors, especially as they, like his work elsewhere, have the benefit of again giving a universal context to the work of other pioneers in this field.

1. The tools of observation, memory, analysis and imagina-tion must, of course, go on developing. It is the actor's body-

awareness which helps in observing others and contemplating just what and how their bodies are both expressing and communicating not just character and characteristics but also feeling, mood and status. The actor has to train the eye for detail and analysis, and this will form the basis of his ideas when creating the role.

2. The actor has also to know and understand the whole instrument of his communication. While this must be an early part of the process, it is by no means a 'one-off' focus of attention but because of its fundamental nature, it involves the actor practising and exploring throughout his lifetime. The actor cannot adequately portray other people unless the instrument for doing so remains tuned and ready.

3. Laban again stresses the two-way nature of movement. The actor has to acquire:

- A development and refinement of external bodily expression – movement affecting inner feeling; and
- A development and refinement of inner movement resources – inner feeling affecting external movement.

The present-day actor has to be physically dexterous *and* be able to communicate the emotional life of each role. Taken separately, either can be a useful starting-point in building a character, though for Laban there is no dichotomy or battle between them since the parts relate to the complete individual and so to the complete roles to be undertaken.

Although actors are quite capable of working abstractly, generally they prefer to train in relation to the concrete and the specific. Laban patterns and principles can easily be presented through specific situations, elements of character or plot.

Outward Physical Approach

As with dance, Laban's outward physical approach turns its attention, at times, to specifics. He does not, however, limit himself to techniques for moving about the stage, but rather sets about freeing the actor and his movement so that he can go in whatever way is appropriate. Practice is given through playing with movement about the space, standing, sitting in a range of positions, timings and intents (as, for instance, with a burglar, a bargain-hunter, a beachcomber, a barman, a bully).

By acquiring skill, for instance, in managing the weight of his own body, he does not have to worry about which foot he is to use or where his gestures should come from or go. Laban's patterns build an inner confidence in finding a 'natural' approach to these external manifestations of the art.

In all kinds of theatre, actors are often called on to vary their outward appearance and Laban principles provide the understanding of the ways in which this can be accomplished effectively (without strain or danger of injury) through detailed work on such areas as:

Posture

First the actor acquires good balance, straight spine, strong abdominals and then it is possible to 'play' with taking the spine in different directions, making different shapes and noticing the effect communicated. Animal improvisations are useful:

- e.g. cat, centipede, chimpanzee, cock, colt, cobra

as is representing a variety of individuals

- e.g. dancer, deacon, dealer, down-and-out, dignitary, doctor.

The actor can experiment with different ways of transferring weight to show postures on the one hand which are more military and formal and on the other more sloppy and informal. The actor has to be able to carry out any of these without stress, being careful to keep as much relaxation as possible even when the posture appears to lack it.

First, different positions of the head, shoulders, arms, hands, pelvis, thighs, knees and feet can be explored, and then discoveries can be applied to particular people and situations:

- an Easter ceremony, the garden of Eden, an electricity cut, an emergency call, an epidemic, espionage, an emotional reunion, an evacuation.

Posture varies with age and/or character and the actor's skill and control should enable rounded shoulders, bent knees, open and closed shoulders, shuffling steps, insecure balance and so on to be conveyed convincingly without undue strain and during offstage times all tensions released and the rhythm of effort and recovery established. Apply to different characters who might be seen:

- at a meeting of the faculty, in a factory, in a family, at a fan club, on a film set, in a flying squad, at a futurist gathering.

Stillness

Stillness is an important part of the actor's art. The body is at rest – neither fidgeting nor rigid – but at that point of control which means the actor feels at ease yet when the body remains as part of the performance. The actor can explore the communication potential of stillness through a variety of people and situations:

- such as: while gambling, on the gallows, in the garden, ghost-hunting, goal-keeping, playing golf, behind the gun, at the grave-side.

Rhythm

Every word, every gesture, every line, action and movement has its own rhythm within the wider rhythm of the scene and ultimately the performance as a whole. Each has its own speed and the subtlety of timing has to work with every aspect of the production.

Body and Vocal Language

Actors can sharpen their awareness by experimenting with the delivery of single words, lines, and their relationship to the action and movement. Begin simply with single words as:

- 'don't', 'easy', 'fire', 'go', exploring different points of stress, pauses before or after.
- Then relate these to gesture and posture, simple action and furious activity. Build them into sentences, sometimes with movement about the space and sometimes from stillness. Observe the nature of the flow and the nature of the rhythm within the flow. Apply this to any given text as a way of discovering its rhythmic potential.
- Build these into a range of situations like: an encounter between mother and daughter, a judge's summing-up, a hostage camp, a tennis match.

Breath and Breathing

For the actor, breath control is important since both voice and movement of the body will require an ample supply and a skilful control of that supply. Playing with the different rates of intake and exhalation, different qualities, and different amounts of projection of the breath into space will not only extend the flexibility and the control but will also make the actor aware of the communication changes which come with these, both in physical and vocal aspects.

Technical skill can be related to characters in specific situations:

- e.g. during a heart attack, in a hallucination, searching for a handkerchief, on a helter-skelter, encountering a major hazard, talking above a helicopter, in a huff, in dire hunger, under hypnosis.

Tension, Release and Relaxation

These go closely in hand with all other work. The actor has

to understand how to relax completely as well as to use tension in the most constructive way, avoiding hypertension on the one hand or a performance devoid of energy on the other. This can be applied to people and situations sparked off by:

- on the ice, the identity parade, the illustrator and the illustrated, imagining some fear, the impenetrable forest, the indoctrinating speech, an indulgent parent, the intermittent sound, my first interview, the irreversible decision.

Coordination

The actor's body needs to be well co-ordinated throughout *and* the voice well co-ordinated with the body. Verbal phrasing and flow will say things about the person and bodily movement has to remain complementary. Confident voices go with confident physical movement; nervous speech is usually accompanied by nervous movement and so on.

The idea of unco-ordination in respect of different situations, characters and states of mind can be explored.

Gesture and Shadow Moves

Both reflect inner experience and need to arise from the role. The first reflects the conscious side of the character, the second the unconscious. Actors can play with gestures and show moves stimulated by such as the following: jailbird, jamboree leader, jazzman, javelin thrower, janitor, Juliet's dream, a juggler's nightmare.

Space Awareness

The actor is using body and voice, so all that Laban offers regarding the body in space and space in the body is pertinent here. Above all, the actor must feel confident and oriented in space. He must be able to 'place' both body and voice where it is most appropriate. Vocally, the space in the body has to be harnessed for tone and projection and the body in the space for the actor's entrances, exits and communication of personality and relationships.

The use of space by both body and voice can be explored in situations arising from such ideas as:

- a Kabuki drama, held in a keep, leaving the kindergarten, every inch a king, flying a kite, a life in the kitchen, living out of a knapsack, the knockabout comic.

Time Awareness

The actor can experiment with different rates of movement, especially with entrances and exits, gestures and travelling about the acting area for different reasons and motivations.

- Direct entrances/exits can be explored along with those that approach the object/space/person indirectly, remembering to give the actor the purpose behind the time change (fear – expressed through slowness or speed, uncertainty, greed).
- These findings might be applied to the long laborious task, the labyrinth encounter, ladies' night, *laissez-faire*, a brief lament, the promised land, the larcenist, my beautiful laundrette, 'you're always late', the laxative, Mr Lazy-bones, liberation at last.

Quality Awareness

Different qualities (light and strong) might also be applied, and rhythms, with different parts of the body taking the lead. (Picking up a bottle of perfume, of beer, of milk, of medicine, of washing-up liquid, of water – performed in a variety of different circumstances, by a variety of different characters.) Throughout, the actor notes the communication effect arising from physical qualities in scenes suggested by:

- the librarian, at the lido, the ineffective weight-lifter, the light-fingered salesman, the day the lightning struck, souls in limbo, 'I've reached my limit', the ever-changing liquid, dealing with holiday litter.

A similar approach can be taken to enhance the actor's awareness of flow, rhythm, and group relationships.

Laban's principles can be applied to physical theatre, where the body speaks louder than the words and where the actor is responding in situations larger than life.

In comedy and slapstick routines, what Laban has to say about relaxation, breathing, balance, rhythm and timing is of great importance. Again, the aim is to build a vocabulary through experimentation. The actor who has already gained control of the physical instrument knows about safety and finds it fun to explore, taking the body on and off-balance in a number of situations such as:

- the trip (over an obstacle, being tripped up) and falling in different directions with different parts of the body leading
- landing in different ways – recovering equilibrium at once, after a stagger, after a roll (forward or backwards), after a slip or slide, after a dive and roll
- the fall – (and 'breaking' the fall) in different directions and from different starting positions (standing, sitting, leaning, walking) and with different dynamics
- pulls, pushes, jumps, kicks, stamps can be similarly explored, different parts of the body leading at different times.

Once the basic dexterity is assured, specific situations will further vary the use of the four motion factors; for instance, an old lady trips over but cannot discover what has caused her to trip. The same happens to a bright young man, a miser, a mystic, a misanthrope, a murderer, a mechanic. It is a hot day, a cold day, evening, midnight, in the city, in the orchard, in open country, in outer space.

Similar approaches help to train the actor for 'serious' physical theatre:

- group and individual making of shapes both abstract and concrete. First experiment with body shapes in relation to the icosahedron as frame of reference. Where can it go, how far can it go (limbs close to and extended from the trunk), what planes can it use, what use can it make of dimensions?
- how can one or more bodies suggest (not necessarily in a literal manner) a door, a tree, a boat?
- how can one or more bodies suggest inner conflicts of different kinds, character changes, contrasts between internal and external responses?

Effort and Character

Laban's work on effort actions can often be a useful road into establishing character, whether for comedy or more naturalistic theatre. Any range of personalities can be developed by experimenting with the creation of:

- people who verbally and physically 'punch', bang, pound their way through life
- people who verbally and physically 'dab', pat or dot their way through life
- people who have a predominance of 'wringing', twisting actions and verbal forms
- people who use 'floating', fondling, enfolding actions and verbal expressions
- people who use 'pressing', bending, stretching, pulling actions and verbal approaches
- people who use 'flicking', sprinkling, picking actions and verbal approaches
- people who use 'slashing', swishing, whipping actions and language
- people who use 'gliding', smoothing, soothing actions and words.

At first, a broad gestural approach might be taken for a generally comic effect. Then the effort actions can be transformed into qualities seen in: posture, foot movements and walking, head movements, movements of the shoulders,

legs. Play with the qualities in the manner of speaking as well
as in the words that are spoken.

Gradually the characteristics can be explored more subtly
so that the whole character, for instance, might 'glide',
gently, imperceptibly undertaking and encountering all
before it letting the same quality of smooth continuous
motion be revealed in voice and speech.

Once the characters are placed in different situations
further discoveries can be made. Several of them can meet:

- at a cocktail party
- at the airport lost luggage office
- after a mugging
- on a weekend art course
- on a package tour
- on an expedition.

Inner Approach – Movement Psychology

> The actor who tries to do more than represent life in a
> skilful manner uses the movements of his body and his
> voice producing organs with his interest focussed on that
> which he intends to convey to his audience and less on the
> external shape and rhythms of his actions . . . A different
> quality of contact with the public results if, instead of skill,
> the inner participation is stressed.[4]

Laban's outline of inner quests relates interestingly to what
followers of Stanislavski have called objectives. But again the
value of Laban's approach is that it is holistic and continues
working out the principle that the actor's sole means of
expression is his body. The motivation may begin from
within or may be stimulated from without, or indeed may be
a combination of the two.

Understanding can be gained by exploring characters with
different inner 'wants', such as:

- to obtain command
- to get married

- to get rich
- to be famous
- to retire.

The process can gradually become more complicated by adding inner resistances:

- envy
- fear
- lack of determination
- poor social background
- low self-esteem.

Then a number of outer problems can be introduced. First, what the character wants to appear, for example:

- as Mr Nice Guy
- as highly sophisticated
- as very self-confident
- as an authoritarian
- as being above worldly ambition.

Then what Laban calls 'outer obstacles' can be introduced and explored such as:

- a person in the way
- the loss of a possible accomplice
- a financial disaster
- a sexual misdemeanour
- peer-group or parental pressures.

Again Laban motion factors can assist in clarifying 'how' these wants and obstacles overcome or are overcome:

- does the character take a direct or an indirect line of action?
- how slow or fast is the character in setting about his/her goals?
- is the approach light (deft) or heavy (strong)?
- is the route free, open, or is it more bound, more controlled?

Some of the ideas mentioned in Laban's *Movement Psychology* can be a useful stimulus for character exploration. For instance, any of the following might be played with in developing a role:

1 A person whose inner attitude exudes:

Stability
Mobility/flexibility/adaptability
Remoteness/aloofness/distance
Nearness/friendliness/closeness/the present
Awakeness/alertness/awareness/vigilance
Dreaminess/unpracticality/living in a fantasy.

2 A person whose externalized drives (internally motivated) might be regarded as:

Doing – seen in his/her desire for action/reacting/exerting
Passion – seen in his/her strong enthusiasm for constructing on the one hand or destroying on the other
Spell – seen in personal attraction of the individual and resulting in either dominating others or surrounding oneself with others
Vision – seen in the person who delights in ideas or facing problems.

Because acting is so bound up with the whole of the human expression and personality, application of Laban's principles knows no bounds. The actor as he interprets each aspect of the human condition is always learning to become more skilful in his adaptation to the physical manifestations of psychological, metabolical and emotional sides of man's being. Likewise he discovers, through his understanding of Laban's patterns and principles, how such aspects of living as:

- the clothing we wear
- the environment we inhabit
- the epoch we live in
- the atmosphere we create
- the specific locality we enter

affect us as individuals and how the body can learn to express and communicate these to onlookers.

For the Theatre Director

The director in the theatre can use Laban approaches to the actor in rehearsing the play. The rehearsal process has to have its rhythm, as should every individual rehearsal. Even if the actors do not have Laban training, rehearsals might be structured to 'play with' movement ideas arising from the script or the overall production concept. What the actors can discover for themselves will be worth much more to the production than that which is superimposed.

Rhythm extends into every sequence/scene/act and to the play as a whole. Scenes can be explored in terms of: tension, flow, pace, dynamic, climax.

The director can use his movement observation, analysis, memory and imagination to work with the actors on such aspects as:

- entrances/exits
- floor and movement patterns
- grouping
- blocking
- characterization
- crowd work
- sustaining spontaneity
- levels.

Laban's principles enable the directorial process to become creative, developmental, collaborative and exhilarating, resulting in lively and effective theatre.

20 Work, Recreation and Worship

(See also Patterns 3–6, 11–14, 15–27, 31–32. cf. also *Effort, A Life for Dance*, and Laban's own experiences mentioned in Ch. 5)

Many of those early experiences in Bohemia helped establish Laban's awareness that the best life was the balanced life and the life that had an integration and a wholeness. He saw a clear connection between work, recreation and worship; in the balanced lives there is a natural rhythm which unites effort and recovery throughout daily existence, giving it harmony. In work, people expend their efforts, while in recreation and worship their efforts should be directed towards the recovery of spent energy and a quest for more spiritual values.

As a child, Laban had seen peasant dances, religious processions and court ceremonials as an integrated part of social existence. He had observed men and women who showed in their movement that they had a pride in their work which was often accompanied by gaiety and song. These folk carried their sense of rhythm into recreation and spiritual expression.

'Man moves in order to satisfy a need.'[5] In work, it may be concerned with those tangible values of lifting, moving, removing, organizing, deciding and so on. In recreation, the need may be larger and more related to the relief of tension or the rechannelling of creative energies, while in religion man's movement expresses his need to unite both with his fellow man and the universal forces which help him to make sense of it all. Nothing confirmed with greater clarity Laban's belief that movement is the common denominator of life and the quality of that life can be seen in the movement.

Work

Of course, the more the individual is in a state of fitness, the more likely he/she is able to respond readily and effectively to the daily work routine. Laban's ideas can be applied to (a) the work we choose to do, (b) being interviewed for the job, (c) how we carry out the work, (d) how we structure the working day, and (e) how we develop self in relation to work.

(a) Movement observation, memory and analysis can help greatly in assessing a person's aptitude for particular areas of work. General observation of movement activity can be linked with observation of shadow movements to help recognize how far an individual's degree of physical co-ordination is developed and how far this is related to their mental co-ordination.

Some individuals will move with greater ease than others and areas of tension can give clues to their capacity for expression of ideas, thoughts and emotions. Whether a person is more comfortable expressing themselves through the physical or the mental can be seen and observation can be made as to which aspects of body, mind and feeling are already given emphasis.

Whether a person tends to move directly or indirectly, lightly or with greater strength, quicker or slower, fluently or more mechanically, can be observed. It is useful too to notice how each person uses space, weight, time and flow. Movement which is predominantly across the body, in the up/down plane or generally forward and back, close to the body or away from it, can be significant and help determine aspects of personality useful in deciding what kind of occupation will suit the individual best. Does the individual tend to open the body or prefer to close in, withdraw, isolate him/herself from others? How the individual organizes his/her movement is important. Is there a natural sense of rhythm?

The carefully trained observer will notice propensity for co-operation, the taking of initiative, responsiveness, sensitivity to others, tolerance, endurance, adaptability as well as capacities to organize both people and things. Such aspects as working best alone or with others can be discerned as well as leadership or following potential. Present capacities can be observed alongside latent possibilities.

(b) Once a person is clear about the kind of job he or she is fitted for, his or her movement will have a strong influence on the impression he or she makes at the interview stage.

Even when interviewers are not trained observers, they are reading, interpreting and often judging an interviewee from the movements they experience. Simple confidence (or lack of it) in entering the room, greeting the panel, taking a seat will have made its impact. Then, throughout the interview, posture, gestures (and shadow movements) and spatial awareness will be communicating to others and will have their effect upon both interviewers and interviewees.

Someone at interview who sits hunched in the chair will have a different impact from the person who leans slightly forward towards the speaker. Furthermore, features like the openness or closedness of the body in conversation will be affecting both auditor and speaker. The mind remains more alert when the body is sitting up and inclined towards the discussion. Avoidance of unnecessary tensions and maintenance of an easy flow throughout the body will work to enable the same qualities to be present in the mind. A well-trained body can convince others of the attractiveness of the personality and the desirability of the applicant at a very early stage in the selection for a particular post.

(c) So many problems occur these days because individuals have not learnt to use their bodies well (and this includes those who use their voices a great deal too) in the tasks that they spend so much of their time carrying out. Laban's approach to tension and relaxation, to effort and recovery are crucial in every kind of daily occupation.

Nearly all jobs require some standing or sitting or walking from place to place. How these simple operations are carried out will affect the well-being of the person. Natural poise (straight spine, strong abdominal wall, firm base at the feet) where the tensions are placed correctly and good balance maintained, will ensure sound use of effort. Likewise, knowing how to manage weight well will enable such tasks as carrying and lifting to be done without strain, whether the particular example is a nurse lifting a patient or a workman digging a trench or an individual carrying a heavy brief case or the household shopping. Without adequate attention to the way the body moves economically, strains and tensions will be built up over a period of time and serious problems will result.

People whose work involves lengthy periods of sitting or standing should build in alternating periods of compensating movement. Drivers need periods of leg and trunk stretching. Those who sit at keyboards for hours at a time need to be observant about the position they occupy in the chair, the position of the head and the relationship between arms, trunk and keyboard. From time to time fingers should be given releasing exercise, shoulders should be opened up and neck and head checked for tensions.

All work which requires a great deal of repetition should have periods of complementary exercise, whether it involves tennis players, violinists, conveyor belt operators or painters and decorators. Laban helped people find their best rhythm for a job by giving them rhythmic movement for the full body even though (or even because) they perhaps spent most of the working day using only part of their limbs.

Because of the two-way process of movement, such activity helps mental as well as physical well-being.

(d) Whenever possible, the working day should be structured around a variety of physical activities. Most work does include routine breaks for tea, coffee, lunch and the like. Better results can be felt if these breaks quite deliberately give the body exercise in compensating directions. It is not always the best way to slouch in an easy chair, inhale a quick cigarette or knock back a coffee and imagine that such 'relaxation' will be adequate. Practising economy of effort in all aspects of work (and breaks in the work) and relating all aspects of work to an overall rhythm are the way to work more efficiently, more effectively and more enjoyably.

(e) Since many people spend the greatest part of their lives in work of one sort or another, it is worth considering the self in relation to that work. Our attention can be given to the way we do the work but we should also pay heed to how we do that work and the effect that it may be having on our personality. Laban's principles can again be applied here. If the physical affects the mental, we should notice the ways in which what we spend so much time doing can set up changes, or reinforce attitudes. It is commonplace that the person experiencing tensions at work brings them home (often unconsciously) in the evening.

Movement awareness can, therefore, assist in helping us to find compensating activities. It can also help us identify weaknesses and strengths both in inner and outer attitudes. Movement activities can be devised on the one hand to release natural movement qualities and rhythms and on the other to help us acquire or learn other skills, qualities, rhythms which seem important for us or for our work. Individuals can work on strength both in body and in mind. Those who wish to gain more directness or indirectness can evolve programmes to help these aspects of their personalities. Understanding Laban's effort qualities will help to identify both strength and weakness in action, and that understanding can form the basis of a programme which can ultimately lead to the growth of a more balanced individual, living and working more in harmony with him/herself.

Recreation

Part of every day, week, month, year can be built into this overall rhythm which leads to this harmony of the individual. The word is itself explicit – bring into existence again, refresh, revitalize. It is for Laban the means for recovery.

Laban observed that earlier generations had found their recovery often by reorganizing the work rhythms and re-experiencing them in dance patterns. So for him dancing remained the great recreational form because in dance there is a tendency for folk to release the tensions and quite naturally find shapes and qualities, rhythms and efforts which complement aspects of personality not given expression elsewhere.

But Laban recognized other forms of recreation too. He recognized that some people wanted to give rein to the competitive element within them and so took part in certain games, or that they wanted to develop skills and aspects of character through setting themselves physical targets and striving towards that kind of achievement or record-breaking.

Those of a more co-operative frame of mind look to working with others on a variety of projects, usually leaving the work-world behind and travelling into small or large group-relationships where they can play together uncompetitively but finding their renewal in this imaginative environment. Often leading out of this approach comes the desire to create something in which they can both express themselves and their ideas and share their experience with others in a communicative performance. Some people choose to devise or interpret a drama, others get together to interpret music or create a dance or dance-drama. Whatever the means, the aim is the same: to refresh the body and mind and to reinvigorate the human spirit.

Worship

When, as a child, Laban had climbed the mountains and, reaching his arms to the sky, had sensed the union with things beyond him, he had been aware of the value of the physical in religious experience and awareness. Simple acts of kneeling for prayer, standing with others and singing forth hymns of praise, were, he could see, only serving to reinforce his belief in the importance of the finite physical being in bringing us in touch with the invisible infinite.

When he observed the Dervishes, Laban realized the power of mind over the body and the body over the mind. He saw that certain shapes and gestures, routines and rituals had their part to play. In the realms of the inexplicable, the movements of the body could give an experience beyond words. Originally, dance was the natural way to *commune* with others and *communicate*. A person dancing often feels that he or she has made contact with a power beyond him or herself, whether it be an archetype or a god or something more inexpressible. We can move to be moved; we can move to identify.

21 Therapy

(See also Patterns 7–10, 12, 14, 18, 19–24, 26, 27)

Amongst that 'string of events' in Laban's path of destiny were several indicators that pointed to the restorative, remedial value that lay in movement, showing how positive and powerful the creative use of it can be. At grass-roots level there had been that growing 'conviction that human beings should be more discerning with their efforts than they generally are.' He saw this to lie in man's neglect of the prime principle of the 'recovery of spent energy'. The result he saw was 'personal exhaustion and misery', not only to the individual him/herself but also to others by 'dragging them into the orbit of disbalanced frenzy.'[6] His observations led him to believe that it was usually because people neglected their regular recreative activities that they had to turn to therapy – and his approach was against the current trend of therapy through words (talking oneself back to balance), but more through deeds, through movement (dancing oneself back to harmony).

Because he also saw what happened all too often through the pressures of modern living and industrialization, he sustained his conviction in a return to open, free, rhythmic, creative liveliness to enable man to restore his dignity, poise and pleasure. It was in the constructive deployment of his sole means of experience and expression – movement – that man could hope to reinstate his sense of wholeness.

He tried out the theory in practice even before the First

World War when he took on the fearfully sick woman in the wheelchair for private lessons. It was a matter first of releasing the tensions in her head and neck, getting her gently, eventually to 'move her shoulders, her arms and her beautiful but rather dead-looking hands.' Wigman was present and noted that after just a few lessons, 'the result was incredible. The sad face lit up again. She dared to move and discovered that she could move. After a while she was able to walk.'[7]

Throughout his life Laban talked about the 'inexplicable influence', of movement and dance, 'both bodily and mentally . . . and . . . its mysterious effects in healing certain illnesses'.[8] His continuing observations enabled him to deepen his understanding and insight. It was not, however, until he reached England and began an association with the Withymead Centre for Psychotherapy that he started more fully to relate his effort theory to their work and especially their basis in the psychology of Carl Gustav Jung.

This exploration in the 1950s enabled him to clarify effort behaviour in terms of individual preferences. He began to develop his theory of moods and drives and to evolve methods for the assessment of personality. Once he had established the relationship between movement behaviour and personality, he could analyse patterns, identify disharmonious aspects and begin the remedial process. Therapy was a matter of using movement for its qualities of healing and growth.

The approach to some extent depends upon the nature of the disorder, though as it is always an approach through movement there are certain basics of theory and practice which are likely always to apply. A similar methodology to that suggested elsewhere is equally sensible here:

1. Observation of current movement and behaviour (both in overt and shadow movement).
2. Analysis of movement in general, predominant efforts used/misused and under-used.

3. Movement employed for rhythm, flow and balance both in expressive exercise and creative execution in order to help restore the balance to the whole personality.

People turn to therapy with all kinds of problems: they may be behaviour disorders or personality problems; the individuals may be having trouble with themselves or finding difficulties in relating to others; the disorder may be largely physical or mainly mental. The deeper and more complicated the problem, the more experienced and specialist-trained the therapist has to be. The good thing about therapy on Laban principles is that it can unite and work with other therapies: occupational therapy, physiotherapy, psychotherapy, and so on. Laban operates from a natural basis that the individual needs to work with, to get to know and gain awareness of the body, and following this he/she gains greater self-awareness (achieving insight about him/herself for him/herself), leading to the restoration of natural harmony of the personality, the wholeness of body, mind and spirit.

1. Detailed and accurate observation is paramount, registering every nuance, gradation and variation in movement activity. This is something of a safeguard against jumping to conclusions. Quite often the process is made more complicated by the fact that it remains important for the person involved in the therapy not to feel that he/she is being observed. The dynamic content of simple actions like picking up a spoon and eating can be noted, for instance, alongside changes in time and whether there is an interchange between flexibility and directness. One can note what parts of the body are used, how and when. Qualities of posture and gesture will also be revealing, as will the various shadow moves that are made. In less functional play, how much free flow and bound flow there is can be noted, together with the individual's sense and use of space, of time changes and which efforts are used and which neglected.

2. In the analysis, it is important to identify tensions. The

place of the tensions, the nature of the tensions, and the degree of tension at different times and in differing circumstances will all help understanding and planning the therapy sessions. Analysis of the movement into various components will lead to their examination for meaning and understanding. Effort patterns can be studied to learn both momentary states of being as well as more general behaviour traits.

Other indicators in the analysis include people's spatial configurations, their sense of balance, of rhythm, range of dynamic and their general involvement with the tactile. All such studies will help to keep the therapist aware of the individual and the uniqueness of each case. It is important to learn how to adapt to changes of mood and mental states as well as different levels at which people can work and the duration of their focus.

3. The actual approach to each person or group has to arise from knowledge, training and experience, but the range of physical activities is enormous. Any bodily action or activity that is expressive, communicative or intuitive (like those suggested in the foregoing sections) can be used in sessions together with sounds and words which of course also form part of the therapeutic movement process.

There already exist many useful techniques in current training practices for both dance and drama which can be usefully employed or adapted, including: exercises in touch and contact; pair and partner work, like mirroring and moulding; making tableaux and tableaux vivants; group games and fun challenges; trust exercises; mimed scenes and improvised scenes with words or sounds; slow-motion actions and accelerated action; playing things larger than life; abstract shapes; and themes based on efforts and effort/ shapes. Good use can be made of free movement to music or percussion or stimulated by an idea, theme or symbol, or at other times the session might be given quite a definite structure or be based around a set of given tasks.

Whatever the approach, the therapist must have a goal

based on the thorough analysis of the individuals in the group. As with other workshops, therapeutic sessions need their continuous critical evaluation of the work to ensure sensible progression in an ongoing growth process. Participants too can step back from the movement process and interpret what they understand was happening in the creative expression. Individuals can speak for the group as well as for themselves. At certain stages they can challenge the group or be challenged by them as well as challenging themselves.

Sometimes the movement therapist will be working alone, sometimes with other specialists. Sometimes movement might be one activity amongst many other therapeutic approaches, sometimes it might be the sole form of the therapy.

Movement therapy is at last finding its followers, researchers, practitioners, trainers and pioneers, and is growing in its application and association. Both in the UK and the USA, there are individuals who delightedly acknowledge Laban, but even those who do not find themselves using Laban's patterns often structure their ideas on his principles. To know more about Laban is not to relinquish anything, but to see the aims and objectives against a broad and universal vision.

Laban is not a panacea, nor a remedy for all our ills. He did not leave a clear statement of his theory for the reason that he knew that no one could ever make a final statement about something that was so fundamental to life – or rather, as he believed, was the essence of life.

What he did say constantly was 'take what you can from my work and make it useful to you, make it yours'. He and many of his followers were well aware that his contributions had to be reinterpreted, were often in need of revision and selection and capable of constant development. He was unafraid to say that he was persistently searching, finding, applying. He was unafraid to declare that exciting discoveries still lay ahead.

But he gave us something quite fundamental to start with, and we should apply the same spirit of adventure in trying to understand and make creative use of it. Once we begin to understand the ideas of Laban, we begin to draw a little nearer to understanding ourselves.

References

Part 1: The Problems in Understanding Laban

1. Joan Littlewood, *Joan's Book*, Methuen, London (1994)
2. Rudolf Laban, *A Life for Dance*
3. Rudolf Laban, 'What has Led you to Study Movement?', *Laban Art of Movement Guild (LAMG) News Sheet*, September 1951
4. Mary Wigman, *The Mary Wigman Book*
5. Rudolf Laban, 'The President's Address at the AGM of the LAMG', *LAMG News Sheet*, January 1948
6. Lisa Ullmann, interview with John Hodgson, June 1971
7. 'The President's Address at the AGM of the LAMG'
8. *A Life for Dance*
9. Valerie Preston-Dunlop, letter, November 1963
10. Lisa Ullmann, interview with John Hodgson, June 1971
11. *The Mary Wigman Book*
12. Rudolf Laban, *The Dancer's World*
13. Mary Wigman and others, 'Tributes to Mr Laban', *LAMG Magazine*, December 1954
14. Kurt Jooss, interview with John Hodgson, October 1973

Part 2: Laban's Ideas in Context

1. 'What has Led you to Study Movement?'
2. *A Life for Dance*
3. 'What has Led you to Study Movement?'
4. *A Life for Dance*
5. *The Dancer's World*
6. Rudolf Laban, 'The Importance of Dancing', *LAMG Magazine*, May 1959
7. Rudolf Laban, *Choreutics Part 1*, ed. Lisa Ullmann
8. Horst Koegler, *Dance Perspectives*, New York (1974)
9. Quoted in Ted Shawn's *Every Little Movement*, Dance

Horizons, New York (1963)

10. Mary Wigman, interview with John Hodgson, September 1973
11. Irene Champernowne, interview with John Hodgson, September 1974
12. ibid.
13. ibid.
14. *The Dancer's World*
15. ibid.
16. Mary Wigman, interview with John Hodgson, September 1973
17. ibid.
18. *The Mary Wigman Book*
19. ibid.
20. ibid.
21. Mary Wigman, interview with John Hodgson, September 1973
22. Kurt Jooss, interview with John Hodgson, October 1973
23. *The Dancer's World*
24. Kurt Jooss, interview with John Hodgson, October 1973
25. ibid.
26. ibid.
27. Fritz Boehme, *Rudolf Laban and the Rise of the Modern Dance Drama*
28. Veronica Sherborne, diary (quoted in *In Memory of Lisa Ullmann*, *LAMG Magazine*, November 1964)

Part 3: Laban's Documented Ideas

1. Kurt Jooss, interview with John Hodgson, October 1973
2. Irmgard Bartenieff, interview with John Hodgson, January 1974
3. *The Dancer's World*
4. Irmgard Bartenieff, interview with John Hodgson, January 1974
5. Rudolf Laban, *Gymnastics and Dance for the Child*
6. Martin Gleisner, interview with John Hodgson, December 1973 and 1975
7. Rudolf Laban, *Choreutics Part 1*
8. F.C. Lawrence, interview with John Hodgson, June 1973
9. Veronica Sherborne, interview with John Hodgson, September 1973
10. Veronica Sherborne, book review in *LAMG Magazine*, November 1964

Part 4: Clarifying Laban's Basic Ideas

1. 'The Importance of Dancing'
2. ibid.
3. Rudolf Laban, 'Movement Concerns the Whole Man', *LAMG Magazine*, November 1958
4. 'The Importance of Dancing'
5. Rudolf Laban, *Mastery of Movement on the Stage*
6. Martin Gleisner, interview with John Hodgson, December 1977
7. *The Dancer's World*
8. *Effort*
9. Rudolf Laban, 'The Rhythm of Effort and Recovery I', *LAMG Magazine*, November 1959
10. Rudolf Laban, *Principles of Dance and Movement Notation*
11. Rudolf Laban, 'The World of Rhythm and Harmony', *LAMG Magazine*, March 1958
12. 'The Rhythm of Effort and Recovery I'
13. *Choreutics Part 1*
14. 'What has Led you to Study Movement?'
15. ibid.

Part 5: Turning Theory into Practice

1. Quoted in L. A. Stone, *Story of a School*, HMSO, London (1949)
2. *Story of a School*
3. *Mastery of Movement on the Stage*
4. ibid.
5. ibid.
6. 'What has Led you to Study Movement?'
7. 'Tributes to Mr Laban'
8. Rudolf Laban 'The Educational and Therapeutic Value of Dance', *LAMG Magazine*, May 1954

Principal Sources

Writings of Rudolf Laban

Choreographie: Erstes Heft (Choreography: Volume 1), Eugene
  Deiderichs, Jena (1926)
Choreutics Part 1, ed. Lisa Ullmann, Macdonald and Evans,
  London (written 1939, published 1966)
'Dance as a Discipline', *LAMG Magazine*, May 1954
'Dance in General', *LAMG Magazine*, May 1961
Denkschrift – über die Ausgestaltung eines Deutschen Tanztheaters
  (Statement on the Setting up of the German Dance
  Theatre), Schloss Banz (unpublished, 1937)
Des Kindes Gymnastik und Tanz (Gymnastics and Dance for
  the Child), Gerhard Stalling Verlag, Oldenburg (1926)
Die Welt des Tanzers (The Dancer's World), Walter Seifert
  Verlag, Stuttgart (1920)
'The Educational and Therapeutic Value of Dance', *LAMG
  Magazine*, May 1954
Effort, with F. C. Lawrence, Macdonald and Evans, London
  (1947)
Ein Leben für den Tanz (A Life for Dance), Carl Reissner
  Verlag, Dresden (1935)
'From Rudolf Laban's Early Writing', *LAMG Magazine*,
  October 1955
Gymnastik und Tanz (Gymnastics and Dance), Gerhard
  Stalling Verlag, Oldenburg (1926)
'The Importance of Dancing', *LAMG Magazine*, May 1959
Laban Art of Movement Guild Magazine 22, 1959 (several
  articles)
Mastery of Movement on the Stage, Macdonald and Evans,
  London (1950)
Modern Educational Dance, Macdonald and Evans, London
  (1948)
'Movement Concerns the Whole Man', *LAMG Magazine*,

November 1958
Movement Psychology, with William Carpenter, (unpublished, 1952?)
Principles of Dance and Movement Notation, Macdonald and Evans, London (1956)
'The Rhythm of Effort and Recovery I', *LAMG Magazine*, November 1959
'The Rhythm of Effort and Recovery II', *LAMG Magazine*, March 1960
'The Rhythm of Living Energy', *LAMG Magazine*, May 1954
Rudolf Laban in conversation with Lisa Ullmann, *LAMG Movement and Dance*, May 1982
'Rudolf Laban Speaks about Music and Dance' (a collection of articles from several *LAMG Magazines*), Addlestone, 1971
'What has Led you to Study Movement?', *LAMG News Sheet*, September 1951
'The World of Rhythm and Harmony', *LAMG Magazine*, March 1958

Writings by Others

Boehme, Fritz, *Rudolf von Laban und die Entstehung des Modernen Tanzdramas* (Rudolf Laban and the Rise of the Modern Dance Drama), unpublished (1949)
Brandenburg, Hans, *Der Moderne Tanz* (Modern Dance), 2nd edition, Munich (1917)
Coton, A. V., *The New Ballet*, London (1946)
Curl, Gordon, *A Critical Study of Rudolf Laban's Theory and Practice of Movement*, MA thesis, Leicester, 1967
Dalcroze, Emil Jaques-, *Rhythm, Music and Education* (trans. H. F. Rubenstein), revised edition, London (1967)
Fordham, Frieda, *An Introduction to Jung's Psychology*, 3rd edition, Penguin Books, London (1966)
Jung, C. G., *Psychological Types, Collected Works 6*, Princeton (1976)
Laban Art of Movement Guild Magazine, Special Birthday Number, 1954
Noverre, Jean George, *Letters on Dancing* (trans. C. W. Beaumont), New York (1968)
Plato, *Timaeus and Critias* (trans. Desmond Lee), Penguin Books, London (1963)
Shawn, Ted, *Every Little Movement*, Dance Horizons, New York (1963)
Stone, L. A., *Story of a School*, HMSO, London (1949)

Wigman, Mary, *The Mary Wigman Book*, Wesleyan University
  Press, Connecticut (1974)

Translations from the German are by Richard Schroder and
  Richard Ellis.

Select Bibliography

Bartenieff, Irmgard, with Lewis, Dori, *Body Movement: Coping with the Environment*, New York (1981)

Berne, E. *Games People Play*, New York, (1964)

Blatner, A. and A., *The Art of Play* New York (1988)

Boehme, Fritz, *Der Tanz der Zukunft* (*The Dance of the Future*), Munich (1926)

Brinson, Peter, ed. *The Ballet in Britain* London (1962).

Bruce, Violet, *Dance and Dance Drama in Education*, Oxford (1965)

Goorney, Howard, *The Theatre Workshop Story*, London, (1981)

Gropius, Walter, *The Theatre of the Bauhaus*, London (1979)

Huizinga, J. *Homo Ludens*, Boston (1955)

Jordan, Diana, *Dance as Education*, London (1938)

Kirby, Michael, ed., *Drama Review* vol. 24 no. 4, *Dance/ Movement Issue*, New York (1980)

Knust, Albrecht, *Development of Laban Kinetography*, in *Movement* (1948).

Koegler, Horst, *Dance Perspectives*, no. 57, (1974)

Krenger, W. K., *Body Self and Psychological Self*, New York (1989)

Lamb, Warren, *Posture and Gesture*, London (1965)

Lamb, Warren and Watson, Elizabeth, *Body Code*, London (1975)

Maletic, Vera, *Body-Space-Expression*, Berlin (1987)

North, Marion, *An Introduction to Movement Study and Teaching*, London (1971)

——, *Personality Assessment through Movement* London (1972)

Piaget, J., *Play, Dreams and Imitation in Childhood*, New York (1962)

Pisk, Litz, *The Actor and his Body*, London (1975)

Preston-Dunlop, Valerie, *A Handbook of Modern Educational Dance*, London (1963)

——*Practical Kinetography Laban*, London (1969)

Ramsden, Pamela and Zacharias, J, *Tapping Management Potential*, Aldershot (1991)

Stanislavski, Constantin, *Building a Character*, London (1948)

Stephenson, Geraldine, *Laban's Influence on Dramatic Movement in The New Era* (1959)

Wethered, Audrey, *Dance and Movement in Therapy*, London (1973)

Wigman, Mary, *The Language of Dance* (trans. W. Sorrell) Connecticut (1966)

Winearls, Jane, *Modern Dance: The Jooss–Leeder Method*, London (1958)

Index

The name of Rudolf Laban appears on most pages of the text. To avoid an overloading of the sections under his name many references to him have been placed under other relevant headings.
Bold figures (**123**) indicate the more important references. 'q' stands for 'quoted'; 'n' directs attention to a footnote.

Index compiled by Frederick Smyth.